KIDS'
ITY COLLEGE
A TO A SMALL
HOUT ANY DEBT.
KEITH W.

GE
EACH OF
ERE
THE
ECEIVED,
OVER
MIKE S.

e during
uated

as difficult,
possible
mmitted

yan M.

My son went to co
college, lived at hom
worked his way thr
He graduated with no o...
and is now saving for a house!
— Beth L.

We
Son, a
cover
but no
and is _debt-free_.

account for our
school to help
y any means,
...cal field
— Cathy R.

THERE ARE SO MANY
GREAT OPTIONS TO AVOID
STUDENT LOANS! DO YOUR
HOMEWORK & HELP YOUR KIDS
UNDERSTAND JUST HOW DANGEROUS
DEBT IS. —TIM A.

I couldn't afford a
four-year school so
I went to a community
college instead. I did all
the prerequisite classes
there and then transferred
to a bigger school as a junior.
It took a while, but I graduated debt-free!
— Laura B.

I walked away with
an MBA & ZERO
debt! It really is
possible to graduate
without student
loans!
— Stephanie J.

DEBT

FREE

DEGREE

All things are possible with God.

MARK 10:27

DEBT

FREE

DEGREE

THE STEP-BY-STEP GUIDE TO GETTING YOUR KID THROUGH COLLEGE WITHOUT STUDENT LOANS

ANTHONY ONEAL

RAMSEY
P R E S S

Published by Ramsey Press, The Lampo Group, LLC
Franklin, Tennessee 37064

This publication is designed to provide accurate and authoritative information with regard to the subject matter covered. It is sold with the understanding that the publisher is not engaged in rendering financial, accounting, or other professional advice. If financial advice or other expert assistance is required, the services of a competent professional should be sought.

Scripture quotations are from the Holy Bible, New International Version®, NIV®, Copyright © 1973, 1978, 1984, 2011 by Biblica, Inc.® Used by permission of Zondervan. All rights reserved worldwide.

Editors: Jennifer Day and Cathy Shanks
Cover Design: Chris Carrico and Gretchen Hyer
Interior Design: Mandi Cofer

ISBN: 978-1-942-121-11-4

Library of Congress Cataloging-in-Publication Data

Names: ONeal, Anthony, author.
Title: Debt free degree : the step-by-step guide to getting your kid
    through college without student loans / Anthony ONeal.
Description: Brentwood, Tennessee : Ramsey Press, 2019.
Identifiers: LCCN 2019023461 | ISBN 9781942121114 (hardcover) | ISBN
    9781942121121 (ebook)
Subjects: LCSH: Education, Higher--United States--Finance. | College
    costs--United States. | College student orientation--United States. |
    College students--United States--Life skills guides. | Parent and
    child--United States.
Classification: LCC LB2342 .O558 2019 | DDC 378.3/8--dc23
LC record available at https://lccn.loc.gov/2019023461

Printed in the United States of America
19 20 21 22 23 WRZ 5 4 3 2 1

This book is dedicated to every young
person who has a dream to go to
college and do it the right way.

CONTENTS

FOREWORD
Dave Ramsey

Not long ago, a high school senior from South Carolina called my radio show. She wanted to know if it was okay for her to attend the University of Mississippi, even though she would need about $50,000 in student loans to cover her out-of-state tuition. After asking her a few questions to dig a little deeper, she finally came clean about why she thought Ole Miss was the school for her.

It's in a really pretty town.

Now, Oxford, Mississippi, *is* a beautiful place, and the University of Mississippi is a fine school. But the truth is, getting a degree from Ole Miss won't do anything to improve her career prospects or increase the income she'll earn after graduation. Instead, she'll be at least $50,000 in debt when she could have received the same education with no debt from almost any state school in South Carolina.

The idea that students can't get a quality education without debt is absolutely ludicrous to me. But far too many people are falling for this myth, and it's ruining their futures. They're carrying a huge burden before they even get out of the gate!

Our culture has become stupid about being educated. That's a dangerous paradox, and it's led to a crushing student loan crisis in America today.

Thankfully, this crisis has produced an overdue wake-up call for many parents—and they're starting to fight back. They're no longer satisfied with letting their kids become student loan statistics. They're refusing to accept mountains of debt or encourage careers that sound fun but offer little to the marketplace.

If you're reading this book, you're probably one of these parents—and I'm proud of you. You're taking an important first step toward avoiding the costly traps of pursuing a college degree. And it's my hope that more parents follow your lead and start counting the cost when it comes to their children's education.

Think about this: along with homes and cars, college is one of the largest financial investments we'll ever make. But when we buy a car or a house, we put in an amazing amount of work. We do research and study options. We analyze every detail before taking that plunge.

But few people perform the same due diligence when picking a school. Somehow college has become an entitlement, and there's no urgency to make intentional decisions or consider the consequences. So families wind up in a financial mess that can take decades to fix!

But here's the truth: You *can* pay cash for college. In fact, you *should* pay cash for college. And I believe this book holds the key to making sure education becomes a blessing, not a curse.

Like all of our Ramsey Personalities, Anthony ONeal provides a clear path that will move you from where you *are* to where you *want to be*. He offers a step-by-step plan, not some stuffy "how-to" guide.

Best of all, Anthony knows his stuff. Over the last decade, he has talked to thousands of American teens. So he definitely understands what makes young people tick. He's also done a ton of research on student loans and college admissions. He knows the most common mistakes people make and clearly explains how you can avoid them.

Unlike a lot of books, *Debt-Free Degree* doesn't just tell you what to do. It gives you a clear path to help your child earn a four-year degree with no debt. And unlike a lot of students, your child will have confidence heading into the real world because they've chosen to connect a common sense plan to their passion.

Look, a college education can have an incredible return on investment. The knowledge and experience it provides are keys to finding real success in life. But a diploma is not some magical ticket. And it's certainly not worth wasting good years and good money paying off student loans. *Debt-Free Degree* will guide you and your child toward wise decisions about education.

This process won't always be easy. Nothing worthwhile ever is. But when things get tough, remember that Anthony and I and the rest of the Ramsey Solutions team stand behind you. We're proud of you for starting this journey. And you can be confident that you've got the best map possible for earning a debt-free degree!

ACKNOWLEDGMENTS

All things really are possible through Jesus Christ. If you would have asked me ten years ago if I would ever write a book, I would have laughed and said no. But God had other plans. He guided my steps here, and I want to say thank you to those who have supported me on this journey:

First and foremost, I want to thank God. I'm a flawed man saved by grace. I don't deserve this opportunity, but I'm grateful for it and I don't take it lightly. Thank you for giving me the chance to love my brothers and sisters.

Dave, Sharon, and the Ramsey family. Four years ago you saw something in me and believed in me. You invited me to join your team and help provide hope to people in all walks of life. I am grateful for your generosity and for the huge shoulders I'm standing on.

Preston Cannon, the book guy (a.k.a. the VP of Ramsey Press). This is our second book and third product in just four years. Wow. Thank you for this opportunity. Thank you for believing in me. Thank you for helping me spread the message.

Matt Litton, you are the man. Thank you for the long hours, late nights, dozens of phone calls, and writing sessions, and for stretching me outside of my comfort zone.

Jennifer Day and Cathy Shanks, my editors. Thank you for making this the best book possible. Let's do some more books together!

Suzanne Simms, Jeremy Breland, and Jim King. From day one of joining this team, you guys have had my back. We've had some tough conversations that have led to an amazing journey. Thank you, thank you, thank you.

The personality team: Rachel Cruze, Christy Wright, Ken Coleman, and Chris Hogan. Watching you win has inspired me to push even harder. Thank you for being the best in your areas and supporting me to be the best in mine. Let's win.

Elizabeth Cole and the publicity team. My desire and dream is to reach all people. Thank you for helping me do just that.

Justin Dorris and Dawn Medley, who handle my speaking and traveling schedule. Thank you for helping me share and spread this message across the nation!

Chris Carrico, Gretchen Hyer, and the design team. The book looks awesome. I'm grateful for your creative eye.

Jeremy Frierson, thank you for donating your time and talent to make sure my wardrobe was on point for the book jacket. Keep going after your dreams.

The AO win team: Lindsey Heatherly, Brad Imburgia, Conner Adams, Connor Wangner, Kelli Porter, Mallory Darcy, Julia Mynhier, Catherine Jackson, Ara Vito, and Kristen Baird. Thank you for dreaming with me, for the disagreements, and for the long meetings. Let's impact a generation!

The entire Ramsey Education Solutions team. Thank you for working every single day to help teenagers graduate high school with the financial literacy that I didn't have. Your hard work is changing the future.

My parents: Anthony and Terry Ross and John and Ann Givens. Thank you for your continued prayers, love, support, and wisdom. I wouldn't be here without you.

Bishop McKissick Jr, the Bethel Church, and One Way—my favorite youth ministry. Thank you for allowing me to serve you and grow with you. My heart for this message began with you.

My nieces and nephews (a.k.a. the chocolate babies). Thank you for loving your uncle. One day you might be in college, and you will do it the debt-free degree way.

All the people who have shared their stories with me. Thank you for helping us learn how to do college the right way.

INTRODUCTION
Proper, Prior Planning

"If you haven't started to plan for college, *you're already late!*"

I'll never forget how I felt when I heard those words: completely blindsided and overwhelmed. It was the last month of my junior year in high school, and I was crowded together with a few hundred other bored students in the Southview High School auditorium for an informational assembly about college. The visitor was from nearby University of North Carolina, and he stood just a few feet away from us on the stage.

As he explained what it would take for us to get into college, my heart sank further and further. While I was trying my best to act like I didn't care, his words had gotten to me like a punch in the gut. All I could think was, *I'm already late?*

Now, I might have looked cool sitting there cutting up with my friends, but on the inside I was completely trippin' out. I was feeling a deep sense of panic, like my future had snuck up on me before I was ready—because it had!

College wasn't a new word or foreign concept to me. I'd thought about it before. My parents always said they wanted me to go to college. In fact, I knew there were twenty-some colleges and universities within driving distance of my house in Fayetteville, North Carolina. I knew all about how prestigious Duke University was. I knew Michael Jordan, James Worthy, and Vince Carter had gone to the University of North Carolina. A lot of my friends had told me stories about colleges like Methodist and Campbell, and Fayetteville State was practically in my own neighborhood.

But that afternoon as Mr. College-Admissions-Expert continued talking, the hard truth started to settle in. I was a few months away from my senior year in high school, and I hadn't had a serious conversation with anyone about college: not with a teacher, not with a guidance counselor, not even with my parents.

He talked about financial aid options . . . and I had never stopped to think about how I would pay for college.

He talked about the ACT and SAT . . . and I hadn't even taken a pretest.

He mentioned how to handle college applications and how to write college essays . . . and I hadn't even made a serious college visit!

He discussed required classes, AP classes, and how we should consider dual-credit courses our senior year of high school . . . and all I had ever considered was how to have a good time *while* getting my diploma!

Now, don't get me wrong: I wasn't a complete slacker in high school. I had really excelled in a debate program and was ranked as the number one student debater in the state of North Carolina. But I also realized that I had spent my entire high school career up to that point focused on *graduating* rather than focusing on the ultimate goal of *getting to college*.

I REALIZED THAT I HAD SPENT MY ENTIRE HIGH SCHOOL CAREER UP TO THAT POINT FOCUSED ON *GRADUATING* RATHER THAN FOCUSING ON THE ULTIMATE GOAL OF *GETTING TO COLLEGE.*

Now, my parents were very involved in my life and wanted what was best for me. But as a parent yourself, you can probably imagine how my parents felt when I came home from school that day: blindsided and overwhelmed, which is *exactly* how I felt too. I didn't know what I was going to do. And because I was their first kid going to college, they didn't know how to help.

That school assembly brought up all kinds of questions about college that my parents and I hadn't considered—questions you and your child can probably relate to. *How in the world was I going to pay for college? How much did it really even cost? What did I want to study? How would I find scholarships? Should I take the ACT or SAT?*

Now, over a decade later, I know firsthand from traveling the country and speaking to students and parents that many, if not most, people have the exact same experience. Most of the parents I meet feel the same way my parents felt. I imagine you might too.

HOW ON EARTH DO WE DO THIS?

It's super exciting that your child is headed to college! It's an awesome goal that will have a tremendous impact on them. But the process of sending a kid to college today is more confusing and expensive than ever. Most parents I talk to don't even know where to start. The process feels mysterious, and they're unsure of even what questions to ask. No one ever sits a parent down and explains, "If you want your student to go to *that* university, then you have to do *this*."

What's worse is the enormous price tag of college. Parents see the cost and think there's no way they can pay cash, so they fall into the trap of believing student loans are the only way. No one tells parents that it's actually possible to pay cash for college. Don't rush past that sentence. *It really is possible to pay cash for college whether you started saving early or it's your student's senior year of high school and you haven't saved a dime.* Your child *can* get a debt-free degree! That's why I wrote this book.

NO ONE TELLS PARENTS THAT IT'S ACTUALLY POSSIBLE TO PAY CASH FOR COLLEGE.

I want you to know what's coming. I want you to know how to pay cash for college! I want you to have a game plan so you know how to navigate the choices you'll face and avoid unnecessary anxiety and ugly financial consequences. The team at Ramsey Solutions and I did our homework to put together exactly what you need to know. Together, you and I are going to build a step-by-step plan to get your student to college—without debt!—and make it a positive experience for you both.

When the team and I began looking at the path to college, we realized quickly it can start early—very early. In fact, some parents begin saving for their child's college education when they're born. If you were able to do that, awesome! You're off to a great start. But for the purposes of this book, let's fast-forward to middle school. That's really the ideal time to get your kid on board and build a college plan that will take them all the way to graduation and beyond.

Now, if you're reading this book as the parent of an older teen—like a junior or senior in high school—you may be feeling really behind. I want you to know you're not alone. Remember, my parents and I didn't start the college conversation until my junior year. Yes, if you're just starting now, it's going to require some creativity to get your child to and through college debt-free—but it *is* possible and we're going to show you how. If you're feeling a little behind, you'll probably be be tempted to jump ahead, but I recommend you read this book all the way through, including those middle school years. You're going to pick up things from those earlier years that will help you and your student lay a solid foundation for the future.

My dad was a distinguished career Marine. He used to tell us something that he learned in the service and adapted to teach my siblings and me. He would say: "Proper, prior planning prevents poor performances!" That has stuck with me and helped me approach all kinds of challenges in my life—and I find it applies perfectly to our discussion about college. I want to help you do the proper, prior planning so you can get your student to and through college—and do it all debt-free!

1

THE WRONG WAYS TO DO COLLEGE

A couple named Jared and Natalie approached me to talk after an event. They had prepared for years to send their first child, Lucy, off to college. They had saved some for school and done a lot of the right things already, but as Lucy neared her senior year of high school, they were completely overwhelmed by their feelings. They hadn't anticipated the emotions they would experience in sending their first child to college. Parents: sending your kid to college isn't easy. And pretending it's *not* hard won't make it any easier. You'll probably feel a lot of anxiety, uncertainty, and grief. My parents actually told me later that the college process was as tough on them as it was on me!

As you work your plan to send your child to college, know that intense emotions are normal. What you want to guard against is making decisions based on those emotions. In addition to anxiety, uncertainty, and grief, the parents I talk to say they feel enormous motivation to help their student. They are *determined* to get their child to college. They're so excited to help them move out on their own for the first time and to become independent adults.

But those same parents also share they feel a good dose of guilt. You know what I mean. It's those feelings that plague every parent: *What if we could've done this? What if we could pay for that? What if we had started saving earlier? What if . . . ?* Now here's the thing: when guilt hits you—along with the resolve to help your student succeed no matter what—it can lead to some pretty bad choices.

Whether you're experiencing guilt, excitement, or anxiety, we need to acknowledge those intense emotions because that's exactly when those financially damaging decisions can start to sound logical, smart even. I've witnessed well-meaning parents take out second mortgages, borrow from retirement, and opt for ridiculous loans because they were reactive and uninformed. Those decisions hurt the whole family for years.

Now, we're going to cover how to pay for college

without debt in Chapter 2, but first we need to talk about the wrong ways to get your kid to college. In my experience, the most stressful part of the college conversation for parents and for students is *always*: "How will we pay for this?" It's usually the first question that comes to mind when college talk gets real. I know this from personal experience. I still remember how the stress levels in my house skyrocketed when I discovered the tuition rates for my college options. And it's only gotten more expensive since then. So let's begin with looking at the consequences of doing it the wrong way: I'll tell you how *I* did it.

MY BIG COLLEGE MISTAKES

During my senior year of high school, my parents and I wrestled with the financial aspects of me going to college. Like I said earlier, I was the first child in our family to go to college, and the truth is that they—like so many parents—weren't really in a position to help me out as much as they would have liked. To be honest, no matter how disciplined you've been with money, unless you've planned for a very long time, it's going to be tough for any parent to pay for the full cost of a college education.

The reality of my situation was that my grades weren't very impressive. I didn't really apply myself in high school. I worked some jobs, but I hadn't saved much. I was fortunate to take advantage of my dad's GI Bill that covered tuition, but I still chose to borrow $10,000 my freshman year for lifestyle expenses like food, trips, and clothes. That's right, parents: student loans aren't just for tuition. Your kid can take out loans for a variety of things during college, including new clothes and spring break vacation, and they don't need your permission or signature to do it. That's one of the reasons loans are so tempting!

So why did I borrow money when I didn't really need to? Because I didn't have a plan for my money or my life. Most of my friends and classmates were paying for college life with student loans and credit cards . . . so that's exactly what I did. The struggle for college kids is real. Taking on debt is ridiculously easy. Way easier than paying all of that money back—with interest.

You know how this ends: just a couple of years later, I owed $10,000 to the big student loan company on top of the $15,000 in credit card debt and $10,000 in furniture store loans I had piled up. I'll never forget when that first payment showed up in my mailbox. My jaw dropped! I owed $500 every month just to repay my student loans. At that point in my life, I was working a job that only paid me about $800 every two weeks. So nearly a third of my paycheck was going to repay my loan from only three semesters in college. Honestly, the decision to take on student debt—to do what everyone else was doing—messed up my financial life for *years*. Don't let your student follow my example: find a different way to pay for college.

STICKER SHOCK

The most shocking difference between when you may have attended college and today is the cost. In 1989, paying for a four-year college degree set you back an average of $26,000. Today, the average total cost for a four-year degree at an *in-state public university* is $100,000.[1] Talk about sticker shock! And the cost is still climbing. From 2008 to 2018, the average tuition and fees for a *private four-year college* went from an already shocking $28,440 per year to $35,830 per year. That's a $7,000 increase for private colleges and universities in only ten years.[2]

It's a tough scenario right now: many of our students need a four-year degree to be competitive in the job market, and yet the cost of college keeps going up. Add to that the fact that tuition increases are far outpacing wage increases. Since 1989, the cost of a four-year degree has grown eight times faster than wages have risen![3] This is exactly why college takes some smart decision-making and long-term planning—and also one of the many reasons to avoid loans.

The Long-Term Cost of Student Debt

The sad truth is that student loan debt is just accepted as normal in today's culture. The reality, however, is that student loans are a significant financial barrier for young people. Student loans keep you or your kid paying for their past when you should both be enjoying your present and future. Today, 70 percent of college graduates walk across that stage with a degree and a truckload of debt.[4] Seventy percent! That means that there are over 40 million Americans who are saddled with school loans, and right now, there is over $1.5 trillion of school loan debt in America. (That's half a trillion *more* in student loan debt than the total US credit card debt!) School loan debt is a national crisis.

STUDENT LOANS KEEP YOU OR YOUR KID PAYING FOR THEIR PAST WHEN YOU SHOULD BOTH BE ENJOYING YOUR PRESENT AND FUTURE.

This honestly makes me really upset. I meet way too many smart, talented young people whose lives are being choked by debt. I'm talking about college graduates who have to live with their parents because they can't afford their own place, can't afford transportation, and can't afford to pursue the jobs they really want because they are drowning in monthly loan repayments. And you know what? A lot of people don't realize that even bankruptcy doesn't usually clear student loans. That debt isn't going away until you pay it back.

So what does all this mean for your child? Let's start with the simple math. If a student borrows $100,000 to pay for school at a 6 percent interest rate, based on a ten-year repayment plan, the "gift" they'll receive after graduation will be a debilitating $1,100 loan payment every month. The current average starting salary for a college graduate is right around $50,000 per year before taxes.[5] That means at least 26 percent of their income (before taxes!) will go to monthly loan payments. And that burden will hang around for at least ten long years, at which point they will have paid the loan company $133,200 in total—that's an extra $33,200 more than they borrowed to go to school!

Now, some students may think, *Wow! Making $50,000 a year sounds great!* But let's do a reality check. Lots of college grads don't make that kind of money coming out of school. Fields like engineering and software development usually pay more than fields like teaching and ministry. (And salary ranges vary widely based on where you live.)

A while back I was talking to a young man from Texas who had recently graduated college with a double major in youth ministry and art. He owed a little over $100,000 in student loan debt and was a teacher. He felt defeated. Student loan debt was not some abstract discussion for him. He was living under this incredible financial burden and had no idea how to pay it off. Listen, y'all, the shackles of debt are very real.

So let's break it down further. Here are the median starting salaries for several different majors:

+ Starting salary for a social work major—$36,483
+ Starting salary for a culinary arts major—$36,200
+ Starting salary for a child development and psychology major—$35,457[6]

What is the monthly reality for a recent college graduate who's making $35,000 a year? How is he going to make ends meet? That's a real good question! It's going to be very, very difficult. A $35,000 salary puts him in the 12 percent tax bracket.[7] Since taxes and insurance will vary slightly from person to person and company to company, let's set his monthly take-home pay at $2,567 after taxes. Now, that may look like a lot of money to a new graduate who hasn't made above minimum wage before, but here's an example of what that kind of income actually looks like in the real world, assuming health insurance is provided through his employer:

Budget 1: Drowning in Student Loans

INCOME	$2,567.00
EXPENSES	
Giving	$0.00
Food	$242.00[8]
Utilities	$200.00[9]
Housing	$1,025.00[10]
Gas/Transportation	$240.00[11]
Car Insurance	$66.00[12]
Renter's Insurance	$0.00
Student Loans	$1,100.00
Car Loan	$0.00
Car Maintenance	$0.00
Credit Cards	$0.00
Cell Phone	$0.00
Health/Doctor's Visit	$0.00
Clothing	$0.00
Entertainment	$0.00
Restaurants	$0.00
Personal Spending Money	$0.00
Birthdays/Christmas	$0.00
Miscellaneous/Unexpected Expenses	$0.00
Savings	$0.00
TOTAL EXPENSES	$2,873.00
DEFICIT	**-$306.00**

Let these numbers sink in. Almost a *fifth* of those with student loans owe over $100,000[13]. But this budget isn't even taking care of what we call the Four Walls—the very basic necessities for living:

1. Food
2. Utilities
3. Shelter
4. Transportation

Because he is swamped with student loan debt, this kid doesn't even have enough to live on, let alone cover some of the fun and responsible stuff like a cell phone, cable, renter's insurance, eating out, putting some in savings, going to the movies, or even buying a birthday gift for Mom.

And did you see that rent amount? The national average for a one-bedroom apartment is 40 percent of his salary after taxes![14] Imagine what happens to your student's finances month after month for ten years when they can't even take care of the Four Walls. Debt robs you of your income every single paycheck.

Now, Budget 1 isn't the worst case, but it's pretty bad. Most graduates don't have quite that much student loan debt, but the principle is the same even for smaller loan amounts. According to the Federal Reserve, the average monthly student loan payment is $393.[15]

Let's look at what happens in a monthly budget with that average student loan payment. To help with rent, let's give our graduate a roommate. That'll bump total housing up to $1,255[16] for a two-bedroom apartment, making his half of rent $627.50. We'll also split utilities but keep his salary the same. Let's also give our grad some other reasonable expenses like savings, car maintenance, and a cell phone. Then, since we're talking about the *average American graduate*, we have to include a credit card and car payment. Here's where it all lands:

Budget 2: The Average American Graduate

INCOME	$2,567.00
EXPENSES	
Giving	$0.00
Food	$242.00
Utilities	$100.00
Housing	$627.50
Gas/Transportation	$240.00[17]
Car Insurance	$66.00
Renter's Insurance	$12.00
Student Loans	$393.00
Car Loan	$345.00[18]
Car Maintenance	$152.00[19]
Credit Cards	$129.00[20]
Cell Phone	$71.00[21]
Health/Doctor's Visit	$30.00
Clothing	$0.00

Entertainment	$0.00
Restaurants	$0.00
Personal Spending Money	$50.00
Birthdays/Christmas	$0.00
Miscellaneous/Unexpected Expenses	$10.00
Savings	$100.00
TOTAL EXPENSES	$2,567.00

Do you see a pattern here? Even with a roommate to help cover rent, this is tough. Still no eating out, no new clothes, and no birthday gift for Mom. Much worse, it will take ten months just to save up $1,000 for emergencies. And we all know what happens when a tire blows and there's not a savings account to pull from: it goes on the credit card. For this graduate, the reality is that it will take eight years to pay off the student loans. This is why many college graduates put off the good things life has to offer like traveling, buying a home, and even getting married.[22] The debt these grads carry makes it really tough to get ahead once they're on their own.

Now, these budgets are just simple exercises that show the real cost of debt. A lot of life will happen during those eight years of paying back student loans. Some of it will be good, like receiving a promotion at work. But some of that life will likely involve additional financial pressure. Unexpected medical bills or a family emergency might pop up. Or the economy tanks and they get laid off.

Life happens all the time but those loan repayments don't quit until you've paid back every last one. As a parent, how hard have you fought over the years to make sure nothing holds your child back? But that's exactly what debt does. It will hold your kid back and rob them of the freedom to say yes to things that come up in the future. We can't predict the future. All we can do is prepare for it. Paying cash for college means you and your child have the *freedom* to make choices that many can't. I know it's easy to take those student loans out initially, but it's going to leave you and your kid in a very difficult position for *years* after graduation.

STRAIGHT TALK ABOUT SCHOOL LOAN FORGIVENESS

Some folks I talk to don't think student loans are such a bad deal because they can be forgiven over time if you follow the right steps. But let me share with you some crazy facts. The requirements for loan forgiveness are demanding. For example, you have to make 120 on-time monthly payments (10 years' worth), only certain types of loans are included, and not every type of payment is counted. Most people who have applied for forgiveness have been rejected.[23]

I met some parents who were incredibly upset about their daughter's student loan situation. Bill and Muriah's daughter, Maya, had attended one of those "close-to-Ivy-League" schools in the South. She had been an excellent student in high school, but this private university didn't give out a lot of scholarships. She took out loans to cover the $65,000-a-year tuition and studied to become a teacher. At the time, it seemed like a good idea, because many of the loans came with the promise of being "forgiven" if she worked in specific areas of education.

Maya graduated with $260,000 in student loan debt and began her career as a teacher earning a starting salary of about $40,000 a year. Her first year out of school, she owed *six and a half times her annual salary* in student loan debt. That's a staggering number when many home mortgages are only three times the owner's annual income.

Now, Maya did everything correctly according to the loan program, including working in the right schools after graduation. But guess what happened when she applied for loan forgiveness? Her application was rejected! Her school debt is financially devastating. She is a phenomenal young teacher making a real difference every day, but she can't afford an apartment or her own car. In fact, she had to move back in with her parents, and she's currently working a night job in order to stay afloat. It's going to take her years to recover financially.

Parents: please make sure your student knows *not* to count on debt forgiveness ever happening. According to the Consumer Financial Protection Bureau, about a quarter of American workers were supposed to be eligible for loan forgiveness—but less than 1 percent of those who have applied for it actually received it.[24]

///

LESS THAN 1 PERCENT OF PEOPLE WHO HAVE APPLIED FOR STUDENT LOAN FORGIVENESS ACTUALLY RECEIVED IT.

///

The promise of loan forgiveness sounds really good, but the reality is it's extremely rare. In order to build a solid foundation for your student, you want to avoid debt at all costs.

THE BABY STEPS AND COLLEGE

What I want you to see in those budgets and hear in Maya's story is how debt hurts you. It doesn't help you get ahead; it limits your options. Now, that's not what you usually hear from colleges, the marketplace, or even the government. And it's certainly not what you see on social media. But that's the reality: the borrower is slave to the lender.

If this is the first time you're considering doing something without debt, you may be wondering if it's really possible. You may even be in a tough financial situation personally and asking yourself if you'll ever be able to get ahead. The answer is a solid yes—*if you do the work to get there*. That's the key: you have to do the work, slowly and steadily.

If you're new to Ramsey Solutions, we teach a simple, proven plan for building lasting wealth. These are the same Seven Baby Steps that our CEO, Dave Ramsey, has lived and taught for almost thirty years. They have led countless people to becoming everyday millionaires, and they will work for you and your student. The Seven Baby Steps are:

1. Save $1,000 for your starter emergency fund.
2. Pay off all of your debt (except the house) using the debt snowball.
3. Save three to six months of expenses in a fully funded emergency fund.
4. Invest 15 percent of your household income in retirement.
5. Save for your children's college fund.
6. Pay off your home early.
7. Build wealth and give.

Each step is important, and the *order* of each step is important. After almost three decades, we have seen over and over that lives are changed when people follow this plan.

Some people get confused and think that our end game is just for everyone to be debt-free. It isn't. Our goal is for people to build wealth and give generously. (That's why we put "Giving" at the top of the budget!) But you can't do that if every month your paycheck is still paying for your past. If you and your child follow this plan, over time you will start to see incredible gains.

So how do the Baby Steps impact going to school debt-free? Well, in addition to staying away from student loans, neither you or your student needs a credit card for college. Not for tuition, not books, not gas, not even as a backup for emergencies. I wish I'd followed that principle in college. Remember that $15,000 of credit card debt I mentioned earlier? Y'all, I bought flowers and a teddy bear for a girl I don't even remember and a ridiculously expensive stereo system for a car that wouldn't even go in reverse! I didn't need any of that stuff! Giving a credit card to a college student is unnecessary at best and stupid at worst.

Now, I know it's common to hear that students need a credit card to build their credit score—but it's just not true. A credit score is only a number that says how much you love debt. It's a calculation of your debt amount, debt payment history, debt type, debt usage, and the likelihood of getting more debt. If you pay with cash, you don't need one. Big Banks will tell you that you *need* a good credit score for things like buying a house, renting a car, or for emergencies. But I'm telling you, you don't.

You can buy a house without a credit score by working with a mortgage company that does manual underwriting. You can use a debit card to rent a car. You can afford to pay cash for an emergency because you've saved an emergency fund full of cash.

Seriously, don't make the mistakes I did. Follow the Baby Steps. Stay out of debt. Teach your student how to pay for their life with cash—including their college education.

The Car Trap

Before we move on, I want to talk about cars for a minute. Parents, your student does *not* need to finance a car. Most people think they can afford a car loan if they can make the payment. But financing a car is like throwing away money. Those people end up paying *thousands more* for a car that's worth *thousands less* the minute they drive it off the car lot. Just like student loans, financing a car is debt, plain and simple. And you can see in black and white what debt does to your student. They don't need student loans. They don't need credit cards. And they don't need a car payment!

Encourage your child to save up and pay cash for their car. It doesn't need to be a super sweet ride. It just needs to be reliable. You can get a reliable car for a few thousand dollars. Then they can save up for a more expensive car, if they want, once they have a decent emergency fund in place.

THE DEBT-FREE DEGREE WAY

The bottom line is, graduating from college debt-free sets your child up for long-term success. Let's run those budget numbers one more time, this time following the Baby Steps, to see what your kid's future looks like without student loans, credit cards, or a car loan:

Budget 3: The Debt-Free Degree

INCOME	$2,567.00
EXPENSES	
Giving	$257.00
Food	$242.00
Utilities	$100.00
Housing	$627.50
Gas/Transportation	$240.00
Car Insurance	$66.00
Renter's Insurance	$12.00
Student Loans	$0.00
Car Loan	$0.00
Car Maintenance	$152.00
Credit Cards	$0.00
Cell Phone	$71.00
Health/Doctor's Visit	$30.00

Clothing	$75.00
Entertainment	$100.00
Restaurants	$60.00
Personal Spending Money	$50.00
Birthdays/Christmas	$34.50
Miscellaneous/Unexpected Expenses	$50.00
Savings	$400.00
TOTAL EXPENSES	$2,567.00

This is some good stuff right here. Graduating debt-free gives your student freedom to use their income to give, save, and live like no one else! With the exact same salary, we were able to *quadruple* the amount of money going into savings, follow the Ramsey teaching of giving 10 percent to church or charities, and start a fund for gift giving so that Mom finally gets a birthday present. You're welcome, Mom.

All joking aside, when your child steps into adulthood without debt, they are positioned to build wealth and build it fast. Just watch: in this scenario, your graduate is a young adult without a house or family, so three months of expenses is probably enough to set aside in an emergency fund. By throwing $400 per month into savings, their emergency fund will be fully funded in just nineteen months. Sweet! Already, less than two years after graduation, your child is covering the Four Walls, has substantial savings, and is ready to start investing while his peers are still struggling month-to-month to pay off student loans.

And think about this: if you remember, the average American graduate will be paying that $393 student loan payment for the next eight years. Instead of being a slave to that payment, if your graduate saves that money over the same time period, they'll be looking at over $37,000. Better yet, if that money is invested in good growth stock mutual funds with an average return of 10 percent, that $37,000 becomes almost $60,000. Then, even if your child never adds another penny to that investment portfolio, that $60,000 will grow to an incredible $1.6 million by the time they hit retirement age. Now, that's what I'm talking about! What's even more amazing is if your child continued saving $393 every month until they retired, their nest egg would be $3 million. That is the power of compound interest over time!

This really hits home for me. When I think about the dumb choices I made as a young person—taking out student loans and falling for credit cards—it hurts me to think how much more money I would have now if I had avoided debt then. That's what I want for your kid!

WHEN TO PAY FOR YOUR CHILD'S COLLEGE EDUCATION

Let's pause for a moment and have a serious conversation about your responsibility as the parent to pay for part or all of your student's college education. A lot of parents put paying for college above saving for their own retirement. *Don't do it!* Like my friend Chris Hogan says, don't put your kids in a position to take care of you financially when you're old because you ran out of money. I know you want what's best for your child, but your *first* responsibility is to make sure your *own* finances are in order. There's a reason we teach the Seven Baby Steps in a particular order. Before you personally contribute to your child's college savings you should

+ be debt-free (except for your mortgage),
+ have a fully funded emergency fund that includes three to six months of expenses, *and*
+ be putting 15 percent of your household income into your own retirement.

If you can do all of that *and* help your student pay for college, then rock on! If you can't, that's okay. You're still a great parent, and you can still help your child. Teach them how they can do this debt-free. Offer them emotional support and guidance. Don't underestimate what a big role you will always play in their lives regardless of how much you contributed financially to college.

Also, don't borrow from your retirement or take out a second mortgage on your house to pay for your kid's college. This is why we have a plan. Even if you're scared out of your mind, stay the course. You really can get your student through college without taking on debt.

One last thing: even if you're able to fully fund your child's college experience, really consider if you should. Allowing them to invest in their college adventure helps them learn more about the value of money and their degree. Remember that we often care more for the things we've worked for than we do for something we're given. There are lots of ways students can get involved in the college process, either financially or with their time. They can work a job during high school and college to help pay for tuition and expenses. They can spend time searching for scholarships. And they can get good grades and prepare thoroughly for the ACT and SAT. Don't do the work for them! Get them invested in this process. It will give them a sense of responsibility and ownership they will draw on for years.

ALLOWING YOUR CHILD TO INVEST
IN THEIR COLLEGE ADVENTURE HELPS
THEM LEARN MORE ABOUT THE VALUE
OF MONEY AND THEIR DEGREE.

A DREAM SCHOOL

Before we talk about specific strategies for paying for college in Chapter 2, we need to redefine a term I often hear misused as I travel the country. As I interact with students, I hear more and more of them talk about their "dream school." They're usually referring to the school they believe will be the most fun, the most prestigious, the one their entire family tree attended, or the one that, in their opinion, will give them the best shot at success. My point to these kids, and one you need to remember, is that the only dream school out there is the one that you can graduate from debt-free!

Blake's story says a lot about how proper, prior planning—even if you start late in the game—can help your student pay for college. Blake did have a dream school. It was the flagship university in his state with a really great national champion football program. He had dreamed of attending that school ever since he was a little boy. It also had one of the better audiovisual production programs in the country, which is what he wanted to study.

Blake didn't really get serious about college until late in his junior year of high school. His test scores weren't great, and he wasn't offered any significant scholarships. Frankly, he was discouraged. As high school graduation approached, he realized he had two options. One, he could take out loans and go straight to his dream school. Or two, he could take advantage of the free community college his state offered. Did he want to go to his dream school his freshman year? Yes! But he chose a better financial future instead.

Blake got after it in community college. He lived at home and completed most of his general education courses with a 4.0 average, all the while working two jobs and saving money. He stayed focused those first two years and was able to transfer to the big state school for his junior year of college. Although he still didn't receive any scholarships or grants, he was able to pay for those two years with cash.

THE ONLY DREAM SCHOOL IS THE ONE THAT YOU CAN GRADUATE FROM DEBT-FREE!

When Blake was offered a paid internship at a television station in New York City after graduation, he was debt-free and financially able to go. Now, several years later, he's an assistant producer for a network and lives in Manhattan with several roommates. His choice to remain out of debt set him up for success after graduation!

Paying for college is not nearly as overwhelming when

you take the time to plan. No matter where you and your student are in the college conversation, I'm going to show you how to pay for college with cash. Your student is going to get their four-year college degree debt-free and will be ready to make a difference in the world without the burden of financial shackles.

YOUR DEBT-FREE DEGREE PLAN

Financial shackles to avoid:

+ Student loans of any kind
+ Relying on debt forgiveness
+ Using credit cards
+ Financing a car
+ Paying for your student's college education before taking care of yourself financially
+ Believing that a dream school is worth any cost

To learn more about getting out of debt, read Dave Ramsey's *The Total Money Makeover*. If you're ready to get out of debt for good, check out *Financial Peace University* at daveramsey.com/fpu.

To learn more about investing, read Chris Hogan's *Retire Inspired*.

2

HOW TO PAY CASH FOR COLLEGE

No matter how perfect a college or university looks, the final decision needs to be based on real dollars and good sense. A college education is one of the most expensive decisions you and your student will ever make. The average annual costs in 2018 for tuition only were:

+ $3,000-$4,000: In-state community college
+ $9,000-$11,000: In-state public university
+ $22,000-$26,000: Out-of-state public university
+ $34,000-$36,000: Private college[25]

Now, in order to get an accurate idea of true cost, you multiply each of these figures by the number of years attended (so usually two years for an associate's degree and four years for a bachelor's degree). Then add on room and board and fees—which varies but averages $10,000 per year.[26] Those are some big numbers!

Rather than letting those numbers paralyze you, let those high costs serve as motivation to get serious about paying for school. In this chapter, we're going to look at a number of strategies to help your student fund college. Keep in mind that every family is different and each situation is unique. As you read through this chapter, look for the steps that match your situation. (For example, your child may or may not qualify for grants.) Then, once you've learned more about each specific step, use the "Your Debt-free Degree Plan" section at the end of the chapter to mark what options will work for your family. This will make it easy to reference your plan as you walk it out.

HOW TO SAVE MONEY ON COLLEGE

There are two main ways to pay cash for college: *saving money* on school and *finding money* for school. So let's dig in to how to save money on college.

Take Advantage of Community College

Now, I know in the past, community college has carried a certain stigma with it. Many have assumed that kids only go to community college because they didn't have the grades to get into a regular four-year school. That's just not true these days. We need to think of community college as the smart way to do college. It's like getting a scholarship without having to write an essay! It's free money!

Remember Blake from Chapter 1? Going to community college saved him $22,000 just on tuition. And because he lived at home during those years, he saved two years' worth of expenses on room and board. That's a serious savings! I love Blake's story because it demonstrates just how powerful community college can be in paying cash for a college education. Even if your child is accepted to a state university, I recommend you at least look into community college options because the savings are big.

EVEN IF YOUR CHILD IS ACCEPTED TO A STATE UNIVERSITY, LOOK INTO JUNIOR OR COMMUNITY COLLEGE OPTIONS BECAUSE THE SAVINGS ARE BIG.

There are a few things your student should pay attention to if they're thinking about community college. First, they want to focus on taking Gen Ed (general education) or prerequisite classes. These are basic courses that most every student has to take to graduate, regardless of what school they go to. It will save good money if they can complete those required classes at a lower cost.

Second, they need to make sure that any hours they take at the two-year school will transfer to their four-year school. I recommend they call the registrar's office and check on course equivalents to make sure the hours they choose will transfer.

Third, consider if taking classes during the summer after high school graduation would benefit them. I know a lot of students who take classes at community college the summer before their freshman year in college to save money and get a head start on credit hours.

Also, you definitely want to find out if your state offers any type of free or reduced college education options. In Tennessee, we have something called the "Tennessee Promise" program. This program allows high school graduates to attend a two-year or technical school free of cost. Now, there are registration deadlines for this opportunity and students have to maintain a certain GPA (grade point average) to keep the scholarship. But there are now seventeen states in the US who have some type of similar Promise program and many others offer reduced tuition. Check into what your state has available.

While we're talking about free, there's another possibility I want to mention called the Modern States Education

Alliance. It's a nonprofit organization that makes first year online education free for students. It's actually called the "Freshman Year for Free" program. It's an awesome option because it allows your student to earn one year of college credit with no textbook or tuition expenses.

Saving Money on Campus

Another way to save money on college expenses is for your student to check out work-study programs or other opportunities for part-time work on campus. The federal work-study program is based on financial need and helps students pay for college through part-time employment. To qualify, you must file your FAFSA (the Free Application for Federal Student Aid, which we'll talk about later in this chapter) and have checked the option on the form that says your student wants to be considered for work-study. It's offered to students as one part of their financial aid package. Now, once your student is offered work-study in their financial aid package, they need to apply for a work-study position on campus. If they get the job, keep in mind that there will be a cap on the work hours granted to your student. But many universities have work-study funds that go unused, so your child could actually ask for more hours, assuming the funds are available. Most students don't know this, and since it's not guaranteed, your child should check directly with the school's financial aid office to see if their school provides this option.

Your student is not limited to jobs based on financial need. There will be a lot of opportunities once they start college—library attendants, teaching assistants, research assistants, working in the mailroom, and even campus barista jobs. The academic services department is also a great place to look. I know of a college in Tennessee that offers discounted tuition for classes if your student volunteers to be a notetaker for students with learning needs. College campuses are a big place, so encourage your student to call the career services office or check the online job boards and apply for positions.

I talked with a young man who attends a private university in Nashville and learned about a program that offers reduced tuition for students who work for the food service company on campus. He told me that his first year he received a 25 percent reduction on tuition, the second year was 50 percent off tuition, and the third and fourth years are a 75 percent discount. All he has to do for those tuition breaks is to maintain his part-time work.

I also talked with a young man named Roberto who is earning his complete tuition bill at a university with a big football program by doing film and social media work for the athletic department there. He only pays for books and housing! This is an incredible savings.

Another great option is to work for the housing department as an RA (resident assistant) in college. This type of position is usually only available to upperclassmen.

It also carries some real responsibility as the job typically requires the RA to be in charge of an entire floor of a dorm or residence hall. But I know of a number of kids who have benefited from being an RA because it usually comes with free room and board. If you just look at the cost of food and housing on most college campuses, this is a substantial cost saver.

Also, be on the lookout for ways to cut back on expenses. For example, a lot of students and parents don't realize they can save money on college meal plans. Bryan was a walk-on athlete at his school. When he registered for college, his parents made sure that his meal plan included three meals every day. He had always eaten three meals a day at home and his parents wanted to be sure he had access to healthy food. Their hearts were absolutely in the right place. But what they didn't take into account was that Bryan wouldn't be on campus seven days a week. He traveled regularly for track and cross country as well as for fun. He also usually ate protein bars or fruit for breakfast in his dorm room. So even though he was an athlete and ate a lot, he didn't need to pay the school for three meals a day, seven days a week.

As you and your student are filling out paperwork and making decisions for freshman year on campus, really think through the options you're offered. If you're not sure what reality will look like, ask a current college student what their experience has been.

HOW TO FIND MONEY FOR COLLEGE

In addition to saving money on college, the biggest resources you and your student have for paying cash for college are scholarships, grants, and savings. Remember, scholarships and grants are free money you don't have to repay. Grants are typically need-based, and scholarships can be based on need or merit. Grants and scholarships are often first come, first serve—so be sure to file your FAFSA and submit your applications as early as possible.

///

SCHOLARSHIPS AND GRANTS ARE FREE MONEY YOU DON'T HAVE TO REPAY.

///

Scholarships and Grants

My friend Jimmy has the best story. His junior year in high school he applied for dozens and dozens of scholarships. When it was all said and done, he figured out that he'd earned $400 an hour filling out scholarship applications! There's no way a high school kid makes that kind of money during their part-time gig at the mall. Listen, working is awesome. There are real benefits to having a part-time job in high school. But in light of how important scholarship money is, seriously consider if your student should look for scholarships and grants as their part-time job rather than working somewhere else.

As your student hunts for scholarships, remind them that they aren't going to get every scholarship they apply for. There are lots of kids applying for these scholarships. And the more money involved, the more applications will be submitted. The key is to apply to as many as possible.

Katie told me her story about the scholarship application process. She had gotten pretty discouraged. By her and her mom's count, she'd sent off forty-two applications for scholarships. It was a lot of work. You know what she had received? Nothing! But she smiled pretty big when she told me the *forty-third* scholarship she applied for at the end of her junior year turned into $28,000 for college. Forty-three applications take a lot of perseverance. Keep encouraging your student to continue applying, no matter how many rejection letters they receive.

Where to Find Scholarships

You're probably wondering where your student finds these scholarships. I want your kid to spend an hour every day searching for scholarships online. To make it easy, I keep an updated list of my top recommendations on my website: anthonyoneal.com. Encourage your teen to start their search there. Keep in mind, there are really three categories of scholarships: academic, athletic, and those based on a student's character.

Now, let's talk about the two types of scholarships available:

1. local scholarships with smaller dollar amounts and
2. national scholarships and grants, which generally offer bigger money contributions.

Local scholarships are actually the best place to start. Because they have smaller dollar amounts, your student will have a better chance at winning them. Why? Well, there are simply fewer applicants. And you know, those smaller scholarships add up. Your student should look into Kiwanis, the Lions Club, banks, utility companies, your local church, area sports clubs, and even your employer. Three hundred dollars here and $800 there will help chip away at paying for school.

I met a college freshman named Mark who was able to cover $4,000 of his tuition simply from local grants and scholarships he received from his church, a local rotary club, and a couple of businesses from his small town. Also, if your student has a part-time job, those companies can be a great place to find scholarships. Chick-fil-A will award over $15 million in 2019 to more than 6,000 team members.

Once your student has exhausted all of the local scholarships they can find, they can start applying for the national scholarships. Now, the national scholarships usually involve more money, but they also bring a lot more competition. I think the Coke scholarship is a good example because they offer $20,000 to 150 students. It's called the "Coca-Cola Scholars" scholarship for high school seniors, and they accept applications for the scholarship between August 1 and October 31 each year.

So what are the odds of your student getting that kind of scholarship? Almost 100,000 people apply for it every year and only 150 are selected. That means the odds are 0.0015 percent! Not real good, right? (Keep in mind, Coke does offer some smaller scholarships as well.) But does this mean your student shouldn't bother with the big national scholarships? Heck no! They should apply for everything they can! We just need to help them understand that the odds are better for the smaller, local scholarship opportunities.

How to Apply

Okay, we've talked about *where* to look for scholarships, now let's look at *how* your student should apply for scholarships. Every college has application windows and deadlines for scholarships. And for most of them there's a list of qualifiers that your student must meet to be considered. Starting in middle school, your child can begin compiling a document of scholarship names, contact info, deadlines, and requirements. Most scholarship applications are completely free. If they aren't, do some research to make sure they're legitimate.

For most scholarships, students will have to write an essay, which will have specific instructions. It's pretty common for students to not follow the directions on these essay assignments, so remind them to follow the writing prompt and word count closely. And be sure to have your child keep every essay they write in a dedicated folder on their computer. Why? Because most of the essay requirements and questions are pretty similar. Students can recycle these essays with a little revision and submit them for multiple scholarships.

Keep in mind that the essays are a big deal. Make sure your teenager sits down with an English teacher, writing tutor, or editor to get help with the first couple of drafts. Essays should be clean, mistake free, and well written.

I talked with a student named Lance who used this strategy, keeping all of his college essays on his computer. When he wrote his first essay at the beginning of his junior year, he got help from a teacher in the writing lab at his school. Once it was edited, he told me he was able to just tweak the essay here and there for other writing assignments. When we talked, he had already used that one essay for fifteen scholarship submissions!

Continue Hunting after College Begins

Here's another thing your student should know about scholarship opportunities: it's still possible to find scholarship money *after* their freshman year in college. The number of students per class on campus generally drops a little each advancing year, so there is naturally more scholarship money and fewer enrolled people applying for those scholarships. Also, many schools will look at your student's first-year GPA in college and value it over what they did in high school—which can be helpful if they've improved their grades since graduation.

I talked with Casey, who attended a state college very close to home for her freshman year. She commuted so she didn't have to pay room and board. She also scheduled her courses for Mondays, Wednesdays, and Fridays so she was free to work on Tuesdays and Thursdays each week. This strategy helped her pay a lot of her tuition. She carried a 4.0 her freshman year and received a full-ride scholarship offer from an out-of-state university that summer.

Though it's certainly helpful if your student can get a head start on their scholarship search in middle school, their efforts should ramp up in high school and continue into college. Ask your teen to make this a daily practice. The earlier they get started and the more scholarships they apply for, the better their chances are for receiving them.

SPECIAL COLLEGE SAVINGS ACCOUNTS

In addition to scholarships and grants, there are a couple of specific ways you as the parent (or even grandparent) can save for and help contribute toward your student's college fund. Assuming you're in Baby Steps 4, 5, or 6, you're ready to take advantage of a couple of special savings accounts designed specifically for education: a 529 and an Education Savings Account (ESA). What makes these accounts unique is that the earnings aren't taxed if used on qualified expenses like tuition, room and board, and books.

Now, there are some differences between the two options, so be sure to do your research to know which one is best for you. Here are a few differences between ESAs and 529s to keep in mind:

COMPARISON	ESA	529
Annual Contribution Limits	$2,000	$14,000*
Income Restrictions for Contributors	$110,000 (single) $220,000 (married)	none
Beneficiary Age Limits	Age 30	none

*Overall contribution to a 529 cannot be more than what your student will use for education expenses, and if you contribute more than $14,000 annually, the funds could be subject to "gift tax." You can check the IRS website for more details about 529 contribution limits.

It's best to start these types of accounts as early as possible because of how they grow over time. Mathematically, if you contribute $2,000 every year to an ESA from the year your child is born until they turn 18, that $36,000— in a growth stock mutual fund that averages a 10 percent return—will turn into over $100,000 by the time they go to school. That will pay for college, folks! And, if your child doesn't need all of that money for their education, under both plans you can transfer the money to a different child as long as they're related to the original beneficiary—like a sibling or even a grandchild. That's quite a legacy to leave for your family.

UNDERSTANDING FAFSA

The last thing we need to talk about in paying for school is FAFSA. It will determine if your student qualifies for federal assistance (the free money—not loans!) and whether your student is eligible for some scholarships and work-study programs. FAFSA is the Free Application for Federal Student Aid, and parents and students have to complete this form every year they attend college. So it's not a one-time deal, but it needs to be submitted before every school year and for each individual child that's going to college. Also, a lot of the early admissions programs require it when making admissions decisions. So potentially it needs to be filled out as early as your student's junior year in high school to impact early admissions and housing decisions.

FAFSA is based on your tax information and determines a dollar amount for what you should be able to pay for college. This information shows how much extra aid you would need for college costs. The form is used to apply for federal student aid, federal grants, work-study, and loans as well as state and college-sponsored aid.

Now, if you can afford to pay outright for the full cost of college, you don't have to file a FAFSA form. But you might want to do it as a backup option. I have a friend whose son was set with a full ride to an out-of-state university. Because college was paid for, the family didn't fill out any FAFSA paperwork. The summer after high school graduation, my friend was diagnosed with cancer and his son decided to stay close to home while his dad went through treatment. While at home, he thought he would take advantage of Tennessee's free community college option but discovered—because they hadn't submitted the FAFSA form—that he wasn't eligible.

If your student is in any way going to depend on grants or work-study programs, or if you want a backup option in case there's a change of plans, make sure your FAFSA is done. And remember: federal *grants* do not have to be repaid. Federal *loans* do have to be repaid and with interest. The FAFSA form is used for both—but we're only interested in financial aid you don't have to pay back.

So now that you have the nuts and bolts of how to pay for college without taking on debt, let's continue building the plan. Starting in middle school, we'll look at the steps your student needs to take each year through high school graduation.

YOUR DEBT-FREE DEGREE PLAN

Look for Ways to Save Money on College

+ Community college
+ Free or reduced online programs
+ Work-study programs
+ On-campus jobs
+ Meal plans

Look for Ways to Pay for College

+ Scholarships
+ Grants
+ 529s and ESAs
+ FAFSA
+ Off-campus jobs

3

MIDDLE SCHOOL: IT'S *NEVER* TOO EARLY TO TALK COLLEGE!

Brady grew up in New Jersey. As a kid, he loved to stare across the Hudson River at all the shiny skyscrapers. He would watch the businessmen in their suits taking the subway to work in the mornings and daydreamed of doing the same someday. Brady was also really good at math and enjoyed solving complex problems. In seventh grade, his middle school hosted an annual career day, and he got to spend a few hours with an accountant on the twentieth floor of one of those giant skyscrapers. Brady would tell you today that those few hours in middle school helped shape his focus for the rest of his life. Nearly twenty years later, he now has a corner office in Manhattan as the Chief Financial Officer (CFO) of a thriving energy company.

Your student's plan to get a debt-free college education begins in middle school for three reasons:

1. Students are *really* impressionable at this age.
2. This is when your student can start making decisions that affect college.
3. It gives you time to plan.

And yes, middle schoolers can be awkward, cranky, happy, childish, adult-like, loud, and quiet—all in the same short car ride. But this is the perfect time to help them start thinking about their future.

CAUTION FLAGS

You know those construction barrels and caution flags you see on the interstate that warn drivers to slow down and help them merge? I need you to picture me right now in construction clothes and a reflective vest waving orange flags like a maniac. Parents, the very first thing we need to do on our middle school plan to a zero-debt college degree is to talk honestly about where a lot of student debt actually comes from. It may surprise you.

I was headed into work one morning and heard a radio show host talking about a conversation he'd just had with the CFO of a private (aka expensive) university in Boston. He asked the CFO about the insanely high cost of college and why our students go into incredible debt. The CFO explained that costs are high, in part, due to the infrastructure of a university—but that there was an even bigger issue to deal with. The biggest problem, according to the CFO, wasn't the high cost of college *but the parents who encourage their kids to go to a school they can't afford!*

WE NEED TO TALK HONESTLY ABOUT WHERE A LOT OF STUDENT DEBT ACTUALLY COMES FROM.

He said what he sees most often is that it's the *parents* who have bought into this idea that the best chance for their student's success is an elite private education. It's the *parents* who are often pressuring their kid to jump through really expensive hoops and take on extreme amounts of debt.

Listen, this may be your most important takeaway of the entire book: your child's future success does *not* depend on an elite education! Your child's success depends on *him* or *her*. In the recent study that Ramsey Solutions did interviewing over 10,000 millionaires, we found that 79 percent of millionaires did *not* attend prestigious private colleges or universities. Let that sink in for a minute. *Almost 80 percent of millionaires built their wealth without a pricey degree.* Your child doesn't need one. Pressuring your student to attend an elite school they cannot afford is the wrong way to go to college. A hundred thousand dollars of debt isn't going to open doors for them—it's going to close them.

YOUR CHILD'S FUTURE SUCCESS DOES *NOT* DEPEND ON AN ELITE EDUCATION!

Now, what if your student wants to go to an expensive school? Should you support them? Only if it's in their best interest. Encouraging an teenager to go $100,000 in debt to get an English degree so they can earn $35,000 a year as a writer is nuts! As Dave Ramsey would say: it's your job as a parent to tell your kid no when they want to make a stupid decision that will wreck their finances for years. Be the voice of reason. Show them the budget breakdowns in Chapter 1 so they can see with their own eyes what their reality will be after college. They won't be able to live on their own. They won't even be able to afford a cell phone! Debt steals your options. Teach them to stay far, far away from it. If your student has a full-ride scholarship to an expensive school, then by all means support them in going! Otherwise, talk them through their debt-free options.

Also parents, I want you to take a moment right now and really consider if college is a dream *you* are pushing on your child or if it's *their* dream. I know a lot of parents who were told as children that they had to go to college, and now they say the same thing to their student out of habit. But it's not true. College isn't for everyone. Not everyone who goes will graduate. Studies show that 40 percent of those who start college don't earn a degree after six years.[27] Let's assume that even half of those folks eventually do finish. That's still a really large number of people who drop out without a degree. Don't push your kids to do something because it's what you wish you had done.

There are incredibly talented young men and women who would be better served going to a trade school, apprenticing under a master craftsman, or going into the military because that's what they're interested in. Everyone is different. We would be in serious trouble if there weren't master electricians or expert military sharpshooters!

Parents, if you and your child are both on board with this college thing, figuring out how to help them do it without debt starts right now. Don't be part of the college debt problem for your student. If college is what they need to reach their goals, show them how to pay for it with cash.

THE POWER OF A DREAM AND A PLAN

Imagine for a minute if someone you loved took you to get a burger in middle school and began a real, honest conversation with you about how you were created to do something meaningful with your life. Imagine if that person would have told you, "You were created for a purpose! You can do anything! And you can go to college *anywhere*!" And then they showed you how to dream and explore and build a plan to make it happen. How would your life have been different? Seventy percent of American adults don't love what they do.[28] Imagine the possibilities if someone had helped you figure out what you loved doing before you ever left home.

Parents, teaching your kid how to dream and plan is a powerful combination. It's like handing them an LED light that will never go out. It will help them find their way for the rest of their life. A good friend of mine is a fantastic elementary school principal for a large city school district. She told me how she helps her very young students begin to dream. Her district was fighting serious problems, including a really high dropout rate. A large number of her students were on free or reduced lunches and only a very few would go on to graduate high school and attend college. So she began a program at her elementary school to take her students on field trips to visit college campuses . . . beginning in the second grade. That's right, she took second graders on college tours! I'm pretty sure people thought she was crazy. But you know what? Over time, a higher percentage of her students began graduating from high school and going on to college.

She explained that her students needed to see the campus with their own eyes, to walk around it with their own two feet. If they could do that, then the idea of college could take root and they could begin to dream about it. If they could imagine it, they were much more likely to do it. She was handing out LED lights. You can do the same thing for your kid.

THE WORLD'S LONGEST PIZZA

The current world record for the longest pizza was made in 2017. It took a group of 100 volunteers 22 hours to make the 1.3-mile-long pizza that included 20,000 pounds of dough, 3,000 pounds of sauce, and 5,000 pounds of cheese.[29] Imagine for a moment a pizza over a mile long— and then ask yourself how you would eat something that big. The answer is, you would eat it one bite at a time.

As we look more in depth at the next six years of college planning, we're going to cover a *lot* of information. It could start to feel overwhelming and even impossible. If this happens to you, I need you to remember: attack this debt-free college process the same way you would eat the world's largest pizza: *one bite at a time*.

There *is* a lot of information here. But remember, our plan covers years of details. If one step starts to feel too big, break it down into smaller steps and do one of those. Little bits of progress over time will add up in a big, big way. Bill Gates said, "Most people overestimate what they can do in one year and underestimate what they can do in ten years." Parents: there is time, and you can do this.

SEVENTH GRADE

Starting in seventh grade you have six years until your student graduates from high school. The best way to build your plan for a debt-free college education is to help them start thinking and dreaming about their future. Most kids don't spend a lot of time doing this.

You can get them started with questions like these:

+ If you could do anything in the world, what would it be?
+ What types of things do you like? What don't you like?
+ What subjects are you interested in studying?
+ What skill sets do you have?

+ What are you naturally good at?
+ What comes easily to you?
+ Do you want to go to college? Why?

The idea here is to start a casual, ongoing conversation. This is low key. There is no wrong answer. The goal is to help them begin to think about what's possible. There are students who never really figure out how much they like science until they discover genetic research. Then, all of a sudden, they pay closer attention in science class and realize how much they enjoy it. Right now, you want to get them thinking about their future and about the possibilities.

Understand your role too. As the parent of your kid, you're with them *a lot*. You've heard their stories and seen them in action. Point out to them what you've noticed. When have you seen them light up? Maybe you saw a new sparkle in their eye during their first school performance. Maybe they came alive as they told you about a math concept they were learning or a poem they were writing. A caring parent who asks questions about the future and calls out the potential they see will help their child begin to see new possibilities.

I met a young woman in Texas named Megan who grew up on a ranch in a small town outside of Austin. No one in her family had ever attended college before, so it really wasn't even an expectation in her house that she would either. But she was fascinated with the female news anchors she saw on television. She loved to write news stories and pretend to be a reporter.

Her dad paid attention to her interests and in middle school, he signed her up for a special summer camp where she got to visit a television station and help make a news program. He showed her what was possible. Years later, she's the first person in her family to ever attend college. She's studying journalism and interning at a local television station. She found her LED light.

Money Talk

While you're having these important conversations with your child, don't forget to talk about money too. Do they know how to make a budget? Have they practiced saving up and paying cash for something they really want? Do they understand what debt is and why it's so harmful? These are such important topics. And if you don't teach them to your kid, our up-to-our-eyeballs-in-debt culture will.

IF YOU DON'T TEACH YOUR KID
ABOUT MONEY, OUR UP-TO-OUR-
EYEBALLS-IN-DEBT CULTURE WILL.

We teach teenagers five basic money foundations at Ramsey Solutions:

1. Save a $500 emergency fund.
2. Get out of debt using the debt snowball.
3. Pay cash for a car.
4. Pay cash for college.
5. Build wealth and give.

If you haven't already, start teaching your kid this year how to manage their money, build wealth, and give generously.

The Duke University Talent Identification Program (Duke TIP)

Seventh grade is also when students can qualify for Duke TIP. The Duke University Talent Identification Program is a nonprofit organization that identifies and serves academically gifted students by providing "above-grade-level testing, enrichment resources, year-round learning options, residential summer programs, online courses, and original research."[30] The program begins as early as fourth grade and goes through the twelfth grade.

Students can join each year during the enrollment period. To qualify, kids must score at or above the ninety-fifth percentile on national standardized tests or 125 or above on an IQ test. (There is also an option for students without access to testing.) A lot of students will qualify in seventh grade based on their test scores from sixth grade. Participating in the program opens up unique learning opportunities as well as potentially helping your student get noticed by colleges.

Jake is the son of one of my coworkers. He qualified for Duke TIP in seventh grade and took advantage of early testing on the SAT (one of the benefits of the program). He scored so well on the SAT that he was invited to attend a three-week summer learning camp and has already received letters from colleges going into his freshman year of high school. The school counselor told his parents that this success, if he continues to work hard, has him on track to earn a full-ride academic scholarship.

What makes Duke TIP special is that it offers a lot of opportunities for your child to explore their interests, it encourages critical and creative thinking, and it puts them around other like-minded students. It's also important to remember that the program extends through high school. So, for example, students in grades 8–11 have the opportunity to spend a weekend at a local university exploring topics not necessarily available to them in high school—like engineering or genetics. Now, what your kid does or doesn't do in Duke TIP in seventh grade isn't going to make or break their college career. Colleges will obviously focus on high school achievements more than those in middle school. Just keep in mind that this is a marathon, and these are small steps you can take to help your kid find their LED light.

EIGHTH GRADE

In eighth grade, we go a little deeper. Those big-picture questions and observations about the future get more specific. Have your student start writing down their ideas and questions in a notebook just for this process, or use the "Debt-free Degree Planning" pages in the back of the book. The goal here is to help your student begin making the connection between what they want to do and what it will take to get there. Here are a few exercises to help you get the conversation started.

Career-minded Talking Points

+ What do you like to do? (Make a list.)
+ What careers match those interests? (Make a list.)
+ Which of those careers do you think you'd do good at and enjoy the most? (Circle one or two.)

Keep in mind this isn't a one-time conversation. Helping your kid think through career options takes time. This is a conversation you need to have at least once a year because it gives them permission to explore new interests. It also takes away any pressure they may feel to know exactly what they want to do this early in the game.

Play the If/Then Game

+ If you want to be a veterinarian (or whatever career they circled), then what education or experience do you need?

+ If you need a four-year degree, then which schools offer programs for that career path?
+ If you want to go to that school, then what's required for admission?
+ If you want to apply, then what classes should you take in high school?
+ If you take the right classes, then what grades do you need to make?
+ If you get accepted, then how much will that school cost?
+ If that's the cost, then how will you pay for it?

///

STARTING THE FINANCIAL PLANNING CONVERSATION EARLY HELPS KEEP THE FUTURE WIDE OPEN.

///

Eighth grade is also the perfect time time to start the money conversation if you haven't done that yet. Discuss if you'll be able to contribute to your student's college costs. Teach them what their options are for paying cash for college and why debt isn't an option. Warn them that they're going to hear from family, friends, and colleges that student loans are the easy way to afford college—but this simply isn't true. Starting the financial planning conversation early helps keep the future wide open. (If you don't start this conversation early, it can end up limiting their options.) Remember, the dream college is the one they can graduate from debt-free.

The Scholarship Search

After you've narrowed the colleges down to a few favorites, ask your child to write them down and put the list where they can see it every day. This will help them stay focused on their future. They can add or subtract schools at any point. Having these schools in mind will help them stay motivated as they start the scholarship search.

A good way to stay organized is to set up a spreadsheet with categories. Your student may need help getting started. Here are some ideas of categories to include:

+ Scholarship Name
+ URL
+ Amount of scholarship
+ Submission deadline
+ Requirements
+ Applied? (Yes or No)

There will be a few scholarships your eighth grader can apply for, but the majority of them are aimed at high school students. Making a list of scholarships early will make applying for them a lot easier later. You may even want to put the deadlines on a calendar so your student doesn't miss out on free money because they forgot to check the list.

Let me give you an example of what early planning can do for your student. Benny grew up surfing, fishing, and swimming on the coast of North Carolina and was always fascinated with the ecosystem around the beach. He knew by the end of his eighth grade year that he wanted to study marine biology across the country in California. He and his parents made a list of his favorite colleges and detailed the cost of each one. Benny actually started working a couple days a week the summer before his freshman year in high school. He also launched his own business washing cars that he continued through high school.

In order to focus on the extracurricular activities that could lead to scholarships, Benny gave up playing sports. Some of his classmates thought he was weird for doing it, but he knew he needed to focus on different priorities to go to his top-choice school in California. He saved the money he made in high school and worked hard both inside and outside the classroom. By his senior year, he had put together enough cash and scholarships to pay for the school at the top of his eighth-grade list. Without that long-term plan, it wouldn't have been possible.

Career Shadowing

In addition to the previous exercises, eighth grade is a prime time to encourage your student to shadow an adult at work. Career shadowing is a powerful way for young people to explore a potential job path. Even if your middle school doesn't offer a formal program, you can help connect your kid to the right professionals. I know a young medical student named Cameron currently doing his residency at a hospital in Alabama. He's working toward becoming a neurologist. He can point back to shadowing a family physician in the eighth grade as the day he decided to become a doctor.

Now, your child may feel shy or reluctant to shadow an adult in their workplace. It can be intimidating for sure, but encourage them that a little preparation and a little experience will help them get more comfortable. Destiny is a young woman in middle school who wanted to work for the FBI. As career day approached, she didn't know how to go about shadowing someone there. Instead, she asked her aunt if she could just shadow her for the day. Her aunt, a journalist in the military, asked a few questions and quickly realized Destiny had zero interest in journalism or the military. So her aunt made a few calls, and Destiny got to spend the day shadowing a woman who worked in the HR department at the FBI. Destiny was stoked.

Before the big day arrived, Destiny's aunt prepped her well. They picked out a professional outfit from her closet. They talked about how to look people in the eye and practiced giving a firm handshake. Destiny even wrote down questions in advance to ask the woman she would be shadowing. When the day came, she was ready for it, and she learned a ton. Proper, prior planning prevents poor performances! A little preparation can go a long way for students.

If your school doesn't have an official program, ask your network of family and friends for any contacts they might have in the careers your child is interested in. Also, keep in mind that career shadowing doesn't always mean spending three hours with a professional at their office. Sometimes it's as simple as you and your student taking that person to dinner and asking them questions you prepare in advance. A colleague of mine was helping his stepson learn more about a career in graphic design. He set up dinner for their family to meet with a talented local designer he worked with, and his stepson gained some very valuable information about how to get his first job as well as what type of college would be most helpful long term.

Practicing for the Big Tests

The last step in eighth grade is practicing for the big tests. Standardized testing—the SAT and the ACT—is a big part of college admissions as well as determining what financial aid your child will qualify for. Preparation for those tests is a huge part of going to college debt-free. You can begin the official pretesting in eighth grade. Now, some students test well naturally, but others need a little more prep. So begin to think through how you can use the pretesting options to your child's benefit.

In the eighth grade, the PSAT 8/9 (or Preliminary SAT) is your testing option. PSAT is the official "practice test" for the SAT. It's a multiple-choice test and considered a great primer for the SAT (and the ACT). The PSAT is generally administered every October in school and there are free sample tests online as well. You can learn more about the PSAT 8/9 at the College Board's website.[31]

Now, just so you know, students usually take the PSAT in October of their sophomore and junior years in high school. PSAT scores from a student's junior year are used to identify National Merit Scholars—an award that can come with some great full-ride scholarship offers. There is also a pretesting option for the ACT, called the PreACT, that is available only to sophomores in high school. The benefit to taking the PSAT in eighth grade is simply to gain experience. It can help your student get comfortable with the style of testing, the rigor of the test, and the way it's administered.

GOING IN FOCUSED

The middle school years are perfect for getting your kid to start thinking about college. And by the end of eighth grade they should understand that it takes a lot of hard work to get there and finish debt-free. By day one of ninth grade, your child should be ready to go in focused, understanding that the next four years will be fun, but that they will also need to work hard. Before they choose their classes for freshman year—usually in the spring of their eighth grade year—they'll need to be thinking about advanced coursework. We'll cover all of that in detail in the next chapter as we look at setting up your student for success in high school.

YOUR DEBT-FREE DEGREE PLAN

+ Help your teen start thinking about their future by asking questions and looking for the early signs of what they're interested in.
+ Help your student connect the dots between the choices they make today and how it impacts their goals and dreams.
+ Ask your student to research any summer camps or workshops they're interested in exploring.
+ Visit nearby college campuses.
+ Make sure you're teaching your child how to manage their money well. Check out *Smart Money Smart Kids* to learn more.
+ Be very clear with your student that debt will not be a part of their plan for paying for college—no matter how much they hear from others that it's the only way.
+ Connect your child with one or more professionals who are doing what your student is interested in.
+ Learn about pretesting options and consider what your student will need to feel prepared.

4

FRESHMAN YEAR ACADEMICS: NOW IT'S ON THE RECORD

It's a dream of mine to one day take my wife and kids to Disney World. So anytime someone tells me how *not* to do Disney, I pay attention. My friend Mike told me once about his family's first trip to Disney World. On their first visit, they just showed up at the park with an entrance ticket in hand. They were super excited but had absolutely no idea what the day would hold.

They spent that week walking endlessly through very crowded parks, moving from one long line to the next in the crazy heat of a Florida summer. They made some nice memories but didn't get to experience many of the rides and shows they'd hoped to. They left feeling a little disappointed.

Now, the second time Mike and his family made the trip, they *planned* the adventure. He and his wife checked out an app that predicted which parks would be most and least crowded each day. They read online articles about which attractions were new and which ones were being refurbished. They worked with a travel agent who specialized in planning Disney vacations and were able to get the best dining reservations. They plotted when to ride certain rides and when to get fast passes for others. They even researched the fastest way to cut through the park to get to their next ride and the best places to stand to watch the parade and fireworks.

All of that research and planning to figure out where they needed to go *before* hitting the asphalt really paid off. At the end of that second vacation, Mike and his family were still exhausted, but they'd seen and done everything they wanted to—and it had been magical.

Listen parents, whether you do the proper, prior planning or not, high school graduation is going to come quickly. Doing the research and planning ahead of time will help your student maximize their time in high school, college, and beyond.

YOUR TRANSCRIPT IS YOUR RESUMÉ

As you look at the big picture of getting your student to college debt-free, remember that your student's transcript is to college admissions what a resumé is to finding a job. Teens need to be thoughtful about what they want their transcript to say to potential colleges. So, for example, you want to make sure your teen's classes fulfill any college requirements for admission. A suggested plan would include:

+ 4 English classes
+ 4 math classes
+ 3 science classes
+ 3 social studies classes
+ 2 foreign language classes
+ 1 fine arts class

As fun as electives like ceramics can be, if your student wants to go to college, make sure they're building a transcript that will serve them in the long run. A strong academic showing is key.

THE GRADES REALLY, REALLY MATTER!

In addition to taking the right combination of classes, students need to focus on getting good grades. Now, I know that sounds obvious, but stay with me. Most students understand that grades are important to get into college and to win scholarships. What most teens don't realize is how those grades matter starting day one of freshman year.

///

MOST TEENS DON'T REALIZE THAT GRADES MATTER STARTING DAY ONE OF FRESHMAN YEAR.

///

Here's why: students apply to colleges during their senior year of high school. What grades do they have to show colleges? Only three year's worth: freshman, sophomore, and junior years. That's it. That means every single class counts—especially their freshman year! If an incoming freshman blows off a class or three, it's going to be difficult to recover.

The way I handled my freshman year of high school really came back to haunt me. I never stopped to think about how my choices would impact my future. I didn't grasp that once you get to high school, it's game on. I ended up failing some courses my freshman year just clowning around. Failing those classes seriously hurt my chance to have a good GPA for the *rest* of high school. I mean, I worked really hard my sophomore year to get good grades, but I discovered that GPAs are a whole lot easier to bring down than they are to bring up—just like it's easy to get into debt and a whole lot harder to get out! My early high school F's made it almost impossible for me to get my GPA back to where it needed to be for college. And those poor decisions limited my college options. Make sure your student understands how critical their grades are starting the first day of high school.

ADVANCED CLASSES

As you think about getting your child to college debt-free, you need to plan on advanced classes. Why? Because colleges want to see that your student challenged themselves. Advanced classes are harder. They usually involve more reading and more assignments. Taking them shows initiative because it's all voluntary!

There are also some added benefits to taking advanced classes. First, it can raise your student's GPA. In a regular class, grades are usually weighted like this:

GRADE	GRADE POINTS
A	4
B	3
C	2
D	1
F	0

In advanced classes, grades are usually worth more because the classes are harder. So an A could be worth 5 points instead of 4, and a B could be worth 4 points instead of 3, and so on. Also, be aware that different types of advanced coursework can be weighted differently. For example, some schools weight an honors class 0.5 point more toward your GPA and an AP class 0.75 point more. As your student makes their class schedule, make sure they know how their high school weights each type of class.

Taking advanced classes also allows your child to be around other high-achieving students. Studies show that if your teenager is placed with other driven students, it can actually help increase their performance.[32] Other benefits usually include smaller class sizes with more discussion and more individualized teacher involvement.

College admissions counselors also understand that honors work is more rigorous, and they pay attention when a student succeeds. In fact, we're even starting to see a shift in how colleges make admissions decisions. In 2018, the selective University of Chicago made the ACT and SAT optional for admissions. This was a huge deal. In an article for *The Chronicle of Higher Education*, University of Chicago's vice president for enrollment, James Nondorf, said, "The transcript tells such a powerful story for us. We went from department to department to see who the stars were. Does testing tell us who's going to be the best art historian? The answer is No."[33] Colleges are paying more attention to a student's choice of classes and grades to predict their success in school.

Now, it's worth saying that just because your kid *can* take all advanced classes doesn't mean they *should*. If your teen struggles with a certain subject, it's fine if they choose not to take that advanced class.

In high school, your options for advanced classes typically include: honors, AP (advanced placement), and dual enrollment. Let's look at each one more closely.

Honors Classes

For most schools, the advanced classes available to freshmen only include honors courses. The main difference between an honors class and a standard class is that they will cover a subject matter way more in-depth. For example, a standard history class may touch on the facts of a historical episode, while the honors class will spend time researching the "whys" behind that same event. Honors classes also move at a faster pace and cover more material.

Now, terminology and scoring for advanced classes can vary between schools. Honors classes are sometimes called *college prep*. Sometimes they are a step above college prep. Make sure your teen asks their high school guidance counselor about the terminology your school uses for the different classes.

A young man named Chet told me how he maintained straight A's his freshman year in some tough honors classes. Those early honors A's raised his GPA more than regular classes would have. His junior year, he took a really difficult AP math class and, even with tutoring and putting in tons of extra studying, he still ended up with a low C in the class. Now, a low C can tank a good GPA, but because of those freshman year honors classes, his GPA was able to withstand the hit. It didn't kill his chances of getting an academic scholarship to college. Freshmen who plan ahead and work their tails off in advanced classes can really set themselves up for success.

Advanced Placement

For the most part, AP classes are open to sophomores, juniors, and seniors. An AP class is roughly the same as an entry-level college course. At the end of it, your student is given the choice to take a standardized exam to earn college credit (or "accelerated placement"). The testing for AP courses is administered by the College Board, a nonprofit founded in 1900 to help students get access to higher education.

Now, the grade you receive from your class and the exam are not tied together. The test is graded on a five-point scale, and you have to earn at least a three out of five to pass. The tests are generally taken in May and sent off to the College Board where thousands of volunteers from across the country work to score the written sections for the test. AP test scores generally come back in July. However, your student can always choose not to take the AP exam at the end of the course.

I talked with a student who received an A from the

coursework in her AP European history class but didn't pass the actual AP exam. Did she waste her time? No, the A she received in the course raised her GPA. She just didn't get college credit for passing the test. The actual AP test has no bearing on your student's GPA, but an AP class does look good to college admissions committees.

The biggest benefit of taking AP courses is that your student can get a head start earning those general education credits in college. If they pass the AP exam, it will save some tuition dollars once they get to college. Keep in mind that individual universities handle AP credits differently—there isn't a set standard. So as you research the schools you're interested in, you'll want to investigate how much credit they will allow your kid to bring into their freshman year.

Dual Enrollment Classes

Dual enrollment courses are college-level courses that are taken in high school. They can be a little more time consuming and rigorous than AP courses because they are often taught by college professors instead of high school teachers. That's a great thing because it will give your child a feel for what college classes are like.

Some high schools only allow students to enroll in these courses *after* they have completed the coursework required by their school district for graduation. This is why understanding the course offerings and planning ahead is critical.

In many cases, these classes are offered by local community colleges or nearby state colleges. They can meet on location at the high school, offsite in an actual college environment, and in some cases, are even offered online. Dual enrollment classes are beneficial because your student is actually taking a college "general education" course like English composition, math, history, or science. It's a great way to get a head start on the coursework required by universities to qualify for graduation.

Although there is a cost for dual enrollment classes, in most cases, your school district or high school covers it if your student passes the class. And having actual college credits on your student's high school transcript is going to give them a huge advantage as they begin to apply to universities. Now, admissions counselors are going to pay close attention to your student's performance in dual enrollment courses, because it's a clear indication of if they can handle the rigor of college coursework. And these kinds of classes can allow your student to try out different subjects and see what "clicks" with them before they even step foot on a college campus their freshman year.

As with AP courses, it's important to check with the colleges or universities on your list to see what credits they allow your student to bring with them. There are actually some universities out there that won't allow your student to transfer AP and dual enrollment credits. And some colleges limit the number of course hours your student can bring in as a freshman. Have your teen do the research ahead of time so they are prepared.

I talked with a young man named Matthew who started planning for college early. His freshman year of high school he enrolled in all the available honors courses. His sophomore year, he started taking AP classes, earned good grades, and was also able to pass the AP tests, which qualified him to receive credit at the state university he wanted to attend. Since he was working on a 5.0 scale, he was able to maintain a really impressive GPA that positioned him in the top fifty students of his graduating class.

Matthew accepted an academic scholarship to an in-state university in the fall semester of his senior year in high school, and the following semester he took two dual enrollment courses offered by his high school and the local community college. When he started college later that fall, he entered a full semester ahead of most of his classmates.

What Matthew accomplished isn't some unattainable goal. It's simply evidence of what your student can do if they're willing to work hard and stick to a plan. Now, all high schools are different. Some don't offer a lot of advanced courses, some do. Colleges understand this. Make the most of whatever opportunities are available to you.

THE WHOLE PICTURE

We spend a lot of time in this book talking about dreaming and planning out your steps, but all of that hard work can be destroyed with one foolish decision. Grades and advanced classes are foundational steps in the plan for a debt-free college education, but equally as important is your student's character—what I like to call their *personal brand*. What is a personal brand? It's what you are about. It's who you really are and what you value. It's what people say about you in your absence. For our students, it's stuff like character, integrity, and loyalty.

Now, why does all this matter for going to college debt-free? Because everything—and I mean everything— is on the record today. Social media means our kids are living their lives on digital platforms and permanently documenting their decisions. This is a big deal because college admissions folks check up on the digital footprint of applicants before admitting them. Not only do their grades matter from day one of their freshman year, but all of their choices do too.

GRADES MATTER, BUT YOUR KID'S
PERSONAL BRAND—THEIR CHARACTER—
IS EQUALLY AS IMPORTANT.

With the far-reaching effects of social media, I teach young people to ask two things when making a decision of any kind:

1. Is this going to get me closer to my goal?
2. Could doing this limit my future?

To put it simply: your teenager's character counts. Let's talk about how this works and what to be aware of.

The Digital Self Is Forever

Do you remember the story about a rookie professional football player who made national headlines? He sent some really offensive tweets, and they ended up being discussed all over the media. Not only did this player have to publicly apologize in a press conference, he had to apologize to his team as well. Apparently, the controversy caused some real problems with some of his teammates. But you know the most interesting part of the story? The tweets from this twenty-two-year-old college graduate were actually made when he was only fifteen years old . . . and he had even deleted them! His poor judgment as a freshman in high school hurt his reputation as a professional years later. Students need to be very aware of their personal brand even in ninth grade!

Your teen is part of the first generation in history to have most of their lives documented in some form or another on social media. The way they handle their digital life impacts their future. When I was a pastor, one of my students shared with me her experience applying to college. She was a smart young woman and the university was considering her for a full-ride scholarship. When the scholarship committee and admissions counselors checked her social media accounts, they found some questionable pictures and posts that didn't reflect well on her behavior outside of school. While it wasn't documented that she lost the scholarship because of her irresponsible social media activity, she did lose the scholarship. A few days later, a counselor from the college who knew the family was kind enough to reach out to her parents "off the record" and direct their attention to her social media posts.

YOUR TEEN IS PART OF THE FIRST GENERATION IN HISTORY TO HAVE MOST OF THEIR LIVES DOCUMENTED IN SOME FORM OR ANOTHER ON SOCIAL MEDIA.

Both college admissions counselors and HR departments are notorious for checking out students and job candidates on social media. It makes sense. Social media can give you a more accurate snapshot of what someone values than a written essay or even a face-to-face inter-view. So let's discuss a couple of things your kid should do to make sure they have their digital presence in order.

First, don't just assume your teen knows how to handle social media. They need your guidance. Sit down with them and go through their existing social accounts (like Facebook, Snapchat, Instagram, and Twitter) and really focus on making sure they reflect good character.

My friend Kenneth is a dad to four teenage children, and he has some sound ground rules for how his teens use social media:

1. Never say anything in a post that you wouldn't feel comfortable reading in front of an entire high school assembly.
2. Never post a picture you wouldn't want displayed in your high school lobby for *everyone* to see.
3. Never post about your feelings. If you're feeling angry or hurt by someone, save it for a face-to-face conversation with friends or family. Social media is not the place to air your personal issues.

Now, what I love about his rules is that they highlight how public and visible social media really is. And, in my experience, students need to be reminded that those little computers we carry around in our pockets are broadcasting something about us to the whole world. Kenneth says these three simple guidelines have helped his kids keep their social media accounts professional and clean.

Second, encourage your teen to create a permanent email address to use for professional contact. When I say "professional contact," I mean this is the email they will use to correspond with colleges, to look for scholarship opportunities, and to communicate with employers. Now, this means they need to lose the juvenile email with the silly handle. Does your kid really want a college admissions counselor or potential employer messaging them at an address like "donothingallday@email.com"? Of course not!

You want to encourage them to be formal with this email address. I recommend helping them set up an account using their first and last name—something straightforward like a.oneal@email is always best. Just remind them that this is a communication tool they'll use for college, work, and professional correspondence for a long, long time.

You're Not Alone

As you and your child build out a plan for high school, remember you're not doing it alone. You'll likely have questions along the way, and both teachers and school guidance counselors can be especially helpful resources.

Encourage your teen to invest time building relationships with their teachers. Remind your kid to treat them like real people. Ask teachers about their day, be polite, be engaged, and be helpful. Most teachers teach because they want to help students. And they can also be very helpful references when your child begins to look for jobs and apply for colleges.

Also, remind your teen to be proactive about asking teachers for help with classwork or homework *before* they need it rather than *after* they get a bad grade. As soon as they feel like they are struggling with a concept, they should ask for help even if it's uncomfortable. I've found the more your student is engaged in their own learning, the more the educators around them will go the extra mile.

Students can also meet with their guidance counselor to ask questions about advanced classes and college admissions. Don't let your student just assume they're on the right track. Your teenager should take ownership of their education to make sure they're completing all of their requirements and in the right order. Have them share their college goals with their counselor, track their coursework together, and ask them about scholarship opportunities.

I would actually recommend that your student see their guidance counselor twice a semester to stay on top of their progress. Counselors are the ones who arrange visits from college recruiters, organize college fairs, and know the costs and requirements of many of the universities that your student may want to attend. They also have knowledge about what college admissions counselors are looking for. Take advantage of their expertise!

NATIONAL HONOR SOCIETY

As you and your student consider your priorities for building a resumé for college, the National Honor Society (NHS) may be a great stepping-stone. NHS is a nationwide organization that recognizes student achievement in high school. It is the oldest and most widely respected student recognition organization in the country. If your student has been involved with the Junior National Honor Society in grades six through nine, they will already know a little bit about the requirements to get into NHS.

The organization only accepts students in grades ten through twelve who have maintained a 3.0 GPA. Because NHS doesn't actually begin for high school students until sophomore year, your student's freshman year grades will determine whether or not they qualify to be part of it.

NHS is more than just an "honor roll group"—it's a service organization. It recognizes achievement in academics, leadership, service, and character. In most schools, the teachers and administrators nominate students for NHS, so it's really a big honor. NHS obviously looks great on college admissions applications, but remind your student that it requires some time and commitment. There are meetings to attend as well as service projects to work on. Your student should join NHS for the right reasons. Volunteer hours because you *want* to serve carry more weight than volunteer hours you *had* to perform to meet a requirement.

IT'S WORTH IT

Academics and character are the foundational elements to your student's college resumé. It will take a lot of commitment and time to do each class justice. There are going to be times when your kid doesn't want to study for another hour or miss the big game of the season. But keep encouraging them that it really will be worth it. They're running a marathon, and each step matters in finishing the race well. And if you or your student start to feel any anxiety about your to-do list, remember that mile-long pizza. Re-read this chapter, break it down, and focus on taking one step at a time.

YOUR DEBT-FREE DEGREE PLAN

+ Focus on building a transcript that will get your student into college.
+ Be relentless about good grades starting day one.
+ Make the most of any advanced classes offered at your high school.
+ Consider AP and dual enrollment classes to help make your student's transcript competitive.
+ Ask the high school what types of advanced classes they offer, the difference between them, and how GPA is weighted.
+ Encourage your teen to get to know their teachers and ask for help before it's needed.
+ Have your student visit their guidance counselor twice a year to: pre-plan and track the right classes in the right order; let them know what colleges your teen is looking at so they can help you meet those requirements; ask them where to look for scholarships.
+ Consider if the National Honor Society is right for your student.

5

FRESHMAN YEAR BEYOND ACADEMICS: THE WELL-ROUNDED STUDENT

It's no secret that, in addition to excellent grades and strength of character, colleges are looking for passion and leadership in students. College admissions and scholarship committees want well-rounded applicants.

Now, notice I didn't say colleges want overcommitted, exhausted students who aim to do it all but have no real identity or direction in life. Parents, this is important. As we dive into Chapter 5, please recognize that I am *not* suggesting your child needs to do every single thing in this chapter. Colleges aren't looking for the student who has done everything.

I read an interesting post on the website for one university about how they choose applicants. Their admissions committee is asking questions like:

+ Has your student been working to capacity in their academic pursuits, employments, or other areas?
+ Do they have initiative? Are they a self-starter?
+ Do they have a direction yet?
+ Do they care deeply about anything?
+ What has your student done with their interests?
+ What is the quality of your student's activities?[34]

Colleges aren't looking for perfect robots. They're not looking for someone with an excessively long college resumé. They're looking for passionate people who will make a strong contribution to their community.

As you and your teen think about life outside of the classroom, remember that their college resumé should reflect their uniqueness. Your student needs to build an extracurricular story that fits them and what they want to do in life. If your fifteen-year-old wants to be an entrepreneur, don't push them to perform in the annual theater production because that's what you did. Help them start a business! If your student loves math and excels in it, encourage them to compete in math competitions—not join the basketball team. For other teens, working part time for a company who will help them pay for college is a great option. And for some students, steadily volunteering at a nonprofit is a better fit. Help your teenager think through what's best for them.

When helping your student decide which activities to choose outside of class, stay focused on these three questions:

+ Does my child enjoy this?
+ Does the activity help them get to their college goal?
+ Do they have time in their schedule to do it well?

EXTRACURRICULAR ACTIVITIES

The first place your student may want to get involved is school-sponsored sports, clubs, and activities. Each high school is different, but there are usually a lot of options to choose from—from the obvious activities like sports and choir to model United Nations, regional art shows, foreign language clubs, mentoring groups, science bowls, and even community service projects.

Now, keep in mind that not *every* club or activity will be part of the path to college. Some can be just plain fun! But their choice of activities shouldn't interfere with college goals. Also, the key ingredient in extracurricular activities is the role your student takes in the group. Colleges are looking for leaders. If they play a sport, then encourage them to be the team captain. They don't have to be the best athlete to be a leader. Or, if they love to talk like I do, they could join the debate club and become the team captain. Their choices of activities should include things they like and show evidence of their best effort.

Now, a word of warning. The biggest mistake I see students make today with extracurriculars is getting involved in way too many activities. We want our student's college resumé to look great, but if your kid is a three-sport athlete, student council member, in the chess club, on the debate team, and an art club member, it also probably means they're spread way too thin! There's not a perfect number of activities to be involved in, just be realistic about your child's interests and time.

Eli is a great example of this. My man Eli was the point guard of his school's freshman basketball team. But as he started looking toward college, he wanted to focus on leadership versus just an activity. He stopped playing for the school and focused on his role as class president of student council and treasurer of a math club. You want to know why this decision was extra tough? His dad was the high school basketball coach! But his dad supported his choice because he knew Eli had a plan. Eli had already determined which colleges he was interested in attending and that he wasn't going to be a college athlete. He wanted to focus his energy on leadership and volunteer opportunities, and he needed to walk away from sports to do that. Eli played ball for fun but threw himself into the things that would get him closer to his goal. You won't be surprised to hear that his tough decision paid off when he received several large college scholarships.

THE BIGGEST MISTAKE STUDENTS MAKE TODAY WITH EXTRACURRICULARS IS GETTING INVOLVED IN WAY TOO MANY ACTIVITIES.

Help your student find the right combination of academics and extracurriculars for them. A young lady named Kennedy chose to give up her leadership role in two other clubs to focus her efforts on volleyball—and it paid off with a full-ride scholarship to a small college. Now, I love sports. I think they are a great way for teens to learn to be part of a team. Sports can teach your student how to work hard, how to win and lose with dignity, and a lot of other valuable life lessons. But I think it's important that you and your teen are realistic about the fact that getting a sports scholarship is rare.

Less than 2 percent of students receive *any* money for playing sports.[35] And not all athletic scholarships cover the full cost of college. One of my coworkers just met with a major SEC school that said they only have half the number of scholarships they need for the size of their team. That means each athlete only gets a 50 percent scholarship. Even if your kid has a real possibility of getting an athletic scholarship, you may need to combine an athletic scholarship with additional academic and merit scholarships.

One last thought about extracurriculars. It wasn't until I got involved in extracurricular activities that I found my groove in high school. As I became successful on the debate and step teams my sophomore year, the discipline and positive attitude I developed there carried over to my academics. In a lot of ways, just understanding what I was capable of accomplishing with a little hard work allowed me to start dreaming about what that could mean for my life. I'm not unique in that way. Studies show that young people tend to do better in school if they're plugged in to activities outside of class.[36] Extracurriculars can help students in a number of ways. Help them choose wisely. Those activities can make a big difference not just in their college planning, but also in their life.

VOLUNTEERING

Another awesome way to be involved outside of the classroom is through volunteer work. Volunteer hours look great on a college resumé, but these service hours are really about learning to serve others well. The purpose isn't to pad your kid's college application. In fact, I believe the time your teenager invests in serving people will benefit them in ways far beyond college. Let me give you an example.

Sarah, a student from a local high school, started looking for a place to do required volunteer hours for a couple of organizations at school. Every day on her way home from school, her bus passed by a retirement home. One day, she asked her parents to drive her over there to see if they had any opportunities to serve. They did, and Sarah ended up volunteering there on Saturday afternoons, playing the piano and helping out with arts and crafts classes. At first, she did it to fulfill community service hours. But something else happened on her Saturday visits: she started to build friendships with some of the residents.

What started out as a pleasant obligation grew into a deeply meaningful experience for Sarah. For four straight years in a row, every Saturday from freshman year through senior year, she faithfully spent several hours of her free time at that retirement home. Those relationships made a lasting impact on her—something far more meaningful than building her college resumé.

My favorite part of her story is that when Sarah gave her speech as the senior class president at graduation, the retirement center had to bring a bus to accommodate all the residents who wanted to attend. As Sarah looked into the crowd during that speech, she realized it wasn't just her family watching, there were three entire rows of elderly friends there to cheer her on. That's rich stuff right there that can only grow out of serving others. If serving others is part of your teen's core motivation, no matter what they choose to do outside of school, they will be successful and happy in life.

Now, a couple of pointers about volunteering: First, as your student looks for opportunities, encourage them to commit to it long term, if possible. Longer commitments usually lead to deeper relationships. Second, it's important that your student documents all of their hours. While college applications aren't the primary motivation to volunteer, your teen will need to provide an accurate account of their volunteer work to admissions counselors. They'll want to track the what, where, and when of their work.

A PART-TIME JOB

Part-time employment can be really beneficial for a student. In some states, fourteen-year-olds can work with a permit, and in others they have to be fifteen to get a job. If your student plans to work, they should max out at fifteen to twenty hours a week. Let's talk about a few of the benefits of maintaining a job through high school.

The obvious benefit to working part time is that your student can start saving money for college. If they begin saving as a freshman in high school, they can put away a lot of money. I know a student who worked her tail off in school: she babysat, worked in a dentist's office, and worked in a restaurant. By the time she went to school, she had made almost $20,000! Working part time also shows colleges that your teenager is responsible, mature, and can manage their time well.

WORKING PART TIME SHOWS COLLEGES THAT YOUR TEENAGER IS RESPONSIBLE, MATURE, AND CAN MANAGE THEIR TIME WELL.

Some employers also offer college scholarships or incentives. Chick-fil-A is a great example. They offer $2,500 college scholarships and a handful of $25,000 scholarships each year. In addition, they have agreements with certain universities around the country to offer employees breaks on tuition. My friend Ryan, who is now an engineer, was able to pay for college with the money he made and the tuition assistance he received working for Chick-fil-A through his high school and college years.

It's never too early to investigate how employers can help your student with their future college plans. Starbucks has a program to cover 100 percent of the tuition for an online undergraduate degree from Arizona State University for their full-time employees. Publix has a great tuition reimbursement program too, and they only require a minimum of 10 hours of work per week to receive that benefit.

I have a friend at work whose son Daniel decided in high school he wanted to get a summer job doing computer programming. His dad told him there was no way anyone would hire a high school kid to program—but he was wrong. Daniel kept talking to folks and landed an internship with a local computer programming company that specialized in technology used in hospitals. Here's the crazy part: not only did Daniel end up working there for the rest of high school, but the company loved him and his work ethic so much they offered to pay for his college tuition if he would commit to coming back and working for them for four years after college graduation. Talk about an incredible opportunity!

Now, if your teen is naturally entrepreneurial, high school is the perfect time for them to start their own business. Being a young entrepreneur shows a crazy level of personal and financial responsibility. But there's a lot to starting your own business. My team and I actually created a guide just for entrepreneurial teenagers called the *Teen Entrepreneur Toolbox*. I love this project because it walks young people through eight easy, practical steps for starting their own business. If you're interested, you can learn more about it on anthonyoneal.com.

I came across a great story about a young man named Justice who wanted to get a job as a freshman in high school, but his choices were limited because he couldn't drive. So he jumped on YouTube and learned everything he could about detailing cars by watching how-to videos. Then he ordered the supplies he needed, along with some business cards, and began to canvas his neighborhood on his bike. He did such an outstanding job on his customers' cars that by the end of ninth grade, he had added two employees to his team to help out with his growing mobile car-detailing business.

By his sophomore year, he was able to buy his own ride with cash, and he expanded his business beyond his neighborhood. By his junior year, he had five employees! He learned how to use QuickBooks, how to pay taxes, and how to handle payroll. When he went to college, he was able to pay cash with the money he saved and the money he continued to earn running his own business. After Justice graduated from his local state college, he kept the momentum going. He flipped his car detailing business into a mobile automotive glass repair company, bought a car wash, then a car lot, and now runs a handful of small businesses in his hometown.

Your teen doesn't have to make their high school business their full-time career after graduation, but Justice's story is a great example of what can be accomplished. Even a simple business mowing lawns in the neighborhood can help your student save money for college and learn to be responsible.

CAREER SHADOWING AND INTERNSHIPS

We talked about career shadowing in Chapter 3, but keep it in mind for high school as well. Career shadowing and internships look great on a college application and will help your student continue to narrow down career options. Some high schools even require documented hours of career shadowing as a requirement for graduation.

I recently met Tyler, who is studying religion in college because he spent a couple of career days shadowing a local pastor. Then there is Hannah, who is studying broadcasting because she had the opportunity to intern at a local radio station during high school. One way to keep expenses down in college is for a student to be focused from the start. (Think about how much money is wasted when a college student switches their major five times and it takes them six years to graduate!) The more your teen can explore career options in high school, the more of a laser beam they can be in college. What excites them right now that's a viable career path? What are they curious about? Those are the areas they'll want to chase down during high school.

KEEP THE END IN SIGHT

Part of keeping your child focused in high school is revisiting the list of questions and colleges they created in junior high. What's changed since they first created their lists? What has your student learned about themselves since then? Are they still interested in pursuing the same direction? Continue refining the list as your student explores different interests.

In addition to their interests and career goals, you need to keep talking with your student about the cost of college and the strategies for how to pay for it with cash. Students will be making their college choice in just two short years, so you need to have some serious conversations about how to pay for it. How much does it really cost? How much, if any, will you as the parent contribute? Has anything changed since you last had this conversation? (It can!) How will they pay for the rest?

Returning to these conversations every few months will help your teen start to narrow down that list of colleges. For example, it's likely the private university that costs $60,000 a year isn't going to be a realistic option without some big-time scholarships. If they dream of attending a state school, they don't need to look at a school in Florida if they live in Tennessee. The in-state institutions are going to be way more affordable. These realizations can help them shape their priorities in and out of school. If they add new schools to their list of colleges this year, remind them to also research the application requirements and costs for those schools.

High school graduation may still seem like a long way off, but it's really only a few semesters away. If your student hasn't begun already, their search for scholarships has to start *now*. Have your teen start building a database of possible scholarships, paying special attention to any scholarships open to freshmen and applying to those. I recommend students look for scholarship opportunities every day during study hall. A kid in my youth group dedicated an hour a day in high school to looking and applying for scholarships—and she earned $88,000 for her education! *Eighty-eight thousand dollars!* Listen, if your kid has time to be on social media every day, I'm going to bet they have time to do this.

Now, there are only a handful of scholarships available for ninth graders, but I met a student named Jared who was awarded a nice scholarship his freshman year of high school. It doesn't hurt to look. As they gather the list of possibilities, they can also begin looking at the types of required essays and begin working with a teacher or tutor to draft samples.

CHOOSE WISELY

It's sometimes easy to lose sight of the big picture when we're in the weeds of this college prep plan. Remember that this process is about a young person's journey to discover their purpose and develop their abilities. It's about setting your student up for success. There's a ton of research that links participation outside the classroom to higher grades and homework completion, and better performance on math, reading, and science tests.[37] In other words, developing yourself outside the classroom helps you develop inside the classroom and vice versa. Help your student choose wisely as they decide how to invest their time outside of class.

YOUR DEBT-FREE DEGREE PLAN

+ Ask your student to make a list of extracurricular activities that interests them. Then go back through the list and prioritize based on level of interest, leadership possibilities, and how much it could help them get to college.

+ Consider if your child should start investing a couple of hours each week volunteering somewhere. Think about long-term options.

+ Brainstorm part-time job possibilities. How can your student start earning and saving money for college? There are some obvious ones here: babysitting, lawn care, pet care, tutoring, car washing. Also consider if your student is interested in starting their own company.

+ Continue to work toward job shadowing opportunities and internships. These are exceptionally helpful for students long term.

+ Periodically revisit your student's interests, career goals, what colleges they want to attend and their requirements, and how they will pay cash for college.

+ Get busy on the search for free money by creating a database of applicable local and national scholarships. Seriously consider working on scholarships for an hour a day, Monday through Friday, each year of high school.

6

SOPHOMORE YEAR: COLLEGE IS CLOSER THAN YOU THINK

Tess was a tenth grader I met after one of my talks. She was doing everything right. She'd absolutely killed it her freshman year of high school. She was involved in band, student council, and had made the Principal's Honor Roll. In her sophomore year, she was on track to be accepted into National Honor Society, taking AP courses to help her knock out college credits and boost her GPA, and a section leader in the marching band. She was focused and engaged. When we talked about her college future, I told her the same thing her band director might say: keep that good rhythm going.

For most sophomores, the main thing they need to know is to continue the good work they started as freshmen. Like I told Tess: they need to keep working hard on academics, keep growing their leadership responsibilities in extracurricular activities, and keep hunting down those scholarships. The amount of scholarships they'll qualify for during their sophomore year is going to be much bigger than freshman year. They need to focus on writing essays and applying for as many opportunities as possible. Being faithful in this can really pay off! Entering the tenth grade is also a good time to do another social media check with your student. Sit down and walk through their accounts together. Remind them to be professional with their social presence and be proactive in building a positive personal brand. Within a year, colleges could be checking out their history on social media.

YOU CAN'T AFFORD TO IGNORE THE TESTS!

In addition to maintaining their rhythm, sophomore year is when you and your student want to really get a handle on the big key tests: the SAT and the ACT. Leyton was a freshman in college when I met him. His story is interesting because he did most of the right things in high school. He was involved in student council leadership, was the captain of the soccer team, carried a 3.8 GPA, and was also a leader on the school spirit team his senior year.

Leyton was accepted to his state school but wasn't awarded any significant scholarships. He was frustrated because he had classmates with much lower GPAs, who were involved in fewer extracurricular activities than he was, yet received $5,000–$6,000 more a year than he did in scholarship money from the college. When we talked through this dilemma, I discovered he'd ignored one of the most important factors in getting a college scholarship: prepping for the ACT and SAT.

Even though some colleges may not put as much emphasis on SAT and ACT scores for college admissions, these test scores are a significant portion of how scholarship awards are decided. Your student can't afford to dismiss these tests if they plan to pay for college with scholarships.

At this point, your student has probably taken the PSAT—maybe even twice. In many school districts, they may have already taken an ACT practice test. If not, they likely will see the ACT pretest early in tenth grade. The first official paid tests don't usually take place until junior year, but *right now* is the time for your teenager to study up and start practicing.

THE COST AND TIMING OF THE TESTS

The ACT and SAT testing actually begins to count for college admissions at the beginning of a student's eleventh-grade year. The absolute latest a student can take one of the tests and still use the score to apply for regular admission to a university is usually January of their senior year. (If they're applying for early decision, the deadline will be earlier.) So the good news is your teen has about a year to prepare to take these tests and to take them multiple times. According to statistics provided by the College Board, almost two-thirds of students who take the ACT a second time are able to improve their overall score on that second attempt (on average by at least one to two points). What's crazy is that statistics show only half of all students choose to take the test more than once. By starting now, your teen has enough time to learn about the tests, which one they should take, and map out a strategy that works for them.

ALMOST TWO-THIRDS OF STUDENTS WHO TAKE THE ACT A SECOND TIME ARE ABLE TO IMPROVE THEIR OVERALL SCORE.

The tenth grade is also when you want to start looking for when and where the ACT and SAT tests will be offered. Your student needs to know the dates and registration deadlines because many of the testing dates can fill up quickly. Those schedules are usually posted online, and your student's high school guidance counselors will also have them.

There's a cost involved with taking both tests. Generally speaking, the costs currently range from $47.50 to $67, depending on whether your student takes the essay portion of the test. (You'll need to know if the colleges your student wants to apply to require the essay section.) Be aware that there is a late registration fee if you miss the regular registration deadline. There can be additional fees as well, like for registering by phone; changing your test center, date, or test subjects; and sending scores to more than four universities. Keep in mind that there are also options available for families who can't afford the testing fees. Check out the websites for each test to find out more: collegereadiness.collegeboard.org/sat for the SAT and act.org for the ACT.

SCORING CONVERSION

Let's go over some of the general facts your student should know about the ACT and SAT. You'll first want to research which test your student's preferred colleges require, if any. Some smaller schools often do prefer one test over the other. It's sometimes even determined by what region of the country you live in. But most major public universities will accept either one.

If your kid has taken both the SAT and ACT tests and wants to submit only their highest score for college admissions, check out the official conversion table provided by the College Board. They've mapped out how scores between the ACT and SAT compare to one another so you know which one is higher. An ACT score of 19, for example, would convert to an SAT score of 990–1020. An ACT score of 22 would equal an SAT score of 1100–1120. A 26 on the ACT would convert to a 1230–1250 on the SAT, and so on.[38]

WHAT'S A GOOD SCORE?

Now, let's briefly review how the tests are scored and what those scores mean. The highest score possible on the ACT test is a 36. The current national average composite score for ACT test takers is a 20.8.[39] So that means that a below-average score is anything lower than a 19, a good score is considered a 20–26, a competitive score would be 24–27, and a top level score is a 28 all the way to the perfect 36.[40] The ACT practice test that's available to most students in the tenth grade can help you get an early feel for how your student will perform.

The highest score possible on the SAT is a 1600. The national average for SAT test takers is a 1050. Below-average scores on the SAT hit under the 910 mark. 910–1200 is a good score, 1200–1400 would be considered competitive, and the top test takers average in the 1400–1600 range. Your child has likely taken the PSAT at this point, so you should have a decent idea of where they may fall right now.

WHAT ABOUT TESTING ACCOMMODATIONS?

Standardized testing can be tough for students with learning disabilities, visual impairment, hearing impairment, or certain medical conditions. Accommodations are available for test takers who qualify, but these requests must be made in advance and documented by your child's doctor.

Accommodations can include things like additional time to take the test, extra or extended breaks, wheelchair-accessible rooms, large font test booklets, the use of a scribe, and alternate test formats. Do your homework early though: it can take a couple of months to receive approval for an accommodation, and then you have to find a facility that can host your teen. (Not all testing sites offer all types of accommodations.)

WHICH TEST IS RIGHT FOR MY STUDENT?

As your child prepares for these big tests, one of your first goals should be to determine which test your student will do better on (assuming they can take either one). The ACT and SAT are different tests: they have different questions and qualities. I think it's helpful to talk with your student about their own learning strengths and weaknesses before deciding which test they should take. Let's look at the profile for the SAT test first.

The SAT Is a Better Match If . . .

The SAT is divided into two major sections. There's a Math Test and an Evidence-Based Reading and Writing section (EBRW). Here are some helpful tips to know if the SAT is the best option for your student:

If your student stresses out about time limits when they're testing, then it's important to know that the SAT offers more time than the ACT. Students who take the SAT observe that it doesn't feel as rushed as the ACT. If your student is likely to freak out about not answering every question, the extra time on the SAT generally allows students to complete every question on the test.

Also, *students who struggle with geometry* want to stick with the SAT because the formulas are provided for the test taker. Not only that, there are fewer geometry questions overall on the SAT.

If your student finds it *difficult to read, comprehend, and remember* where the answer to a question may be located in a reading passage, they may find the SAT questions easier. The SAT actually tells the test taker which reading lines they should review in order to find the answer.

Now, if your student *loves to write essays in English class*, the SAT essay format is more like a typical class writing assignment. It requires your student to read, analyze, and respond to a specific passage just as they do in their high school English class.

If your student *doesn't like science,* they're in luck because the SAT doesn't even have a science section! There are some science-related questions on the test, but not a separate section dedicated to science like on the ACT.

The ACT Is a Better Match If . . .

The ACT is divided in clear sections by discipline: English, math, reading, science, and the optional writing section. Here's what you need to know when considering the ACT for your student:

There's less time available to complete the questions for each section of the ACT. The test requires better time management overall. You want to *make sure that your child works well under pressure and can manage their time* if they're going to choose the ACT. A shorter test can also be appealing and motivating to some kids.

If your student struggles with vocabulary, the ACT may be a better choice between the two tests. The SAT actually has a more challenging vocabulary level.

The ACT requires test takers to recall and find information without being told where to look. *If your student has really strong reading comprehension skills,* meaning that they can read, comprehend, and then remember where something is located in a passage, they will likely do well.

The ACT is organized by subject matter. *So if your student prefers subject-focused tests*, where all the math questions are in one section, all of the science questions are in another, and so on, they will prefer the ACT.

If your student loves geometry or trigonometry, there are more of these questions on the ACT. It's important to remember that the ACT requires those formulas to be memorized (the SAT provides them in the test questions). Your student will also be able to use a calculator for the math section of the ACT.

Unlike the SAT, the ACT has a science section. *If your student does well in science*, this section could really help boost their score.

Finally, *if your student prefers to share their opinion in writing*, the ACT essay sections are more focused on having them explain and defend their opinion like a persuasive writing assignment. It isn't the usual English paper format that requires your student to respond to a reading passage.

HOW TO IMPROVE TEST SCORES

When you think about the SAT and ACT tests, I want you to think of them more like a strategy game. It is possible for your student to raise their scores, and there are a number of tutoring services and books that specifically address how to do so. We'll cover some of this in Chapter 8, but here are a few initial pointers.

There are a ton of practice tests available to your student online. Some are timed to simulate the real tests and some aren't. These can be helpful, but ask your teenager's guidance counselor which they recommend because there are some low quality and ineffective practice options out there.

I definitely recommend exploring test prep courses. Some research shows students can increase their score up to four points on the ACT and 100–150 points on the SAT. This can make a big difference in admission and scholarships, but keep in mind not all students will improve this much. Be wary of really big claims from test prep companies, and check with your school administrators, psychologists, or guidance counselors for their recommendations.

WHAT IF YOUR STUDENT DOESN'T DO WELL?

The truth of the matter is that there are a lot of bright and successful students who are just straight-up bad at testing. I once talked to a student who would literally memorize her notes from class word for word and still do poorly on her exams. It wasn't a lack of preparation or motivation. She just didn't perform well on tests.

Maybe that's your student. So what do you do if your student doesn't do well on these tests? What if they take it several times and just don't score well? Can they still go to college? The answer is *yes*. There are many state schools and community colleges that will admit students with lower standardized test scores.

Open admissions, or open enrollment colleges and universities, accept students with high school diplomas, GEDs, or the equivalent. You can apply to open enrollment schools without taking an ACT or SAT test. Many of these schools also offer remedial courses for students who aren't ready for full college-level coursework. And here's another option: there's a small but growing trend of schools who are beginning to place a higher value on essays and high school grades for admission and scholarships. So it's not impossible to find a good college scenario for your student if they had good grades but didn't perform well on the tests. Just because they can't win at the testing game doesn't mean your student can't win at college. The one thing lower test scores usually impacts is the number of scholarship awards they will win. So take this into account as you consider how to pay for college.

JUST BECAUSE THEY CAN'T WIN AT THE
TESTING GAME DOESN'T MEAN YOUR
STUDENT CAN'T WIN AT COLLEGE.

ENJOY THIS YEAR!

As crazy as it sounds, college is only about two years away for your sophomore! You and I know just how fast that time will go. Help your teenager stay focused on the end game. Sophomore year is about maintaining a good pace inside the classroom. And outside, it's about hunting for scholarships and preparing for the big tests. It's also a really fun year of high school and the last year of calm before the college storm. College activity ramps up in a serious way junior year, so enjoy the slower pace of tenth grade with your child.

YOUR DEBT-FREE DEGREE PLAN

+ Keep the rhythm your student established freshman year. Focus on getting good grades and exploring interests and leadership opportunities outside of academics.

+ Encourage your teen to hunt and apply for scholarships every day.

+ Research what tests your student needs to apply to their preferred schools and what scores they'll need for admissions.

+ Talk through the differences between the ACT and SAT with your student and if they have a preference for which one to take.

+ Investigate test prep courses and which one might be right for your teen. Ask for recommendations from the guidance counselor and from other parents about what course worked well for their student.

+ Plan a time for your child to practice taking the ACT and SAT tests. The goal is for them to get comfortable with the tests.

7

THE X's AND O's OF
THE BIG TESTS

If you've spent any time around football, you've likely
heard the expression "the X's and O's of the game." It
refers to the diagrams coaches draw on their chalkboards
to teach players a new play. X's stand for the defensive
team and O's for the offensive team. Every coach will tell
you that the way to win any game is to understand the
X's and O's, or the fundamentals of success.

In this chapter, we're going to take a closer look at
the "X's and O's" of the ACT and the SAT. These big
tests are usually key steps in your student's plan to go to

college debt-free. It's hard to win scholarships without a good score! We're going to drill down into the details of each test, so you and your student can learn more about how to approach them. And then we'll talk a little bit about superscoring—what it is and how it can benefit your student and change their test prep strategy.

I met some parents whose experience reflects how important it is to learn *everything* you can about these tests before junior year when they matter for your student. Their twin sons, Dylan and Noah, were outstanding students and athletes. Their parents explained to me that they were pretty competitive with each other and would push each other to be better in all areas. They also excelled in similar ways academically. Both did well in math and science classes. So it came as a surprise to their parents when the twins scored very differently on the ACT and SAT pretesting.

Dylan performed really well on the PSAT, but Noah didn't. Noah scored really well on the ACT pretest, but Dylan struggled. Because the boys always had similar academic strengths, their parents were interested in what was going on. They spoke to the guidance counselor, the school psychologist, and even went to see a testing specialist. They learned as much as they could about the tests and decided to encourage their boys to focus individually on the test they each had early success on. When the real testing arrived their junior year, the lessons they'd learned in the pretesting held up.

While the two boys had similar academic strengths, they approached testing differently. Noah, who was a slower and more methodical test taker, scored high enough to qualify for academic scholarships on the SAT, but didn't perform as well on the ACT. And Dylan, who was much better at managing his time and approached testing with a quicker method, scored much higher on the ACT.

Two very similar students still had to choose the test that best suited them in order to get the highest scores possible. I share this story because it shows how important it is to not only take both tests (or at least their pretests) but to really dig deep and learn about each test as well. Paying attention to the pretesting, consulting professionals, and helping your student prepare for the right test really does make a difference.

Let's cover a few things before we dive into the logistics of the testing options. First, like we discussed previously, both the ACT and the SAT cover the same general topics. They both also hold the same level of rigor. And both of the tests were designed to help determine whether or not your student can be successful at the college level—although they approach this from different angles.

So what's the main difference in approach? Well, the ACT is a measurement of what your student already knows. It's designed to cover material that your student should have learned during their time in secondary school education. The SAT is meant to be more of a predictor of what your student is capable of learning. In other words, it's designed to measure your student's skill level more than assessing what material they learned in high school. These are the big-picture philosophies behind how the tests are designed—even though the test questions on each test may be similar. Now, let's take a closer look at the ACT.

A CLOSER LOOK INSIDE THE ACT

The ACT is divided into four required sections and one optional section. Keep in mind that all of the questions except for the essay are multiple choice with four answer options for each question. Here are the following sections of the ACT:

The first section of the test is *English* and that section has *75 questions*. Your student will have *45 minutes* to complete this section that includes reading passages with underlined phrases and questions about writing style, grammar, punctuation, or some other aspect of writing.

The next section of the test is *Math*. It contains *60 questions* covering arithmetic, algebra I and II, geometry, trigonometry, probability, and statistics. Your student will have *60 minutes* to complete this section and they are allowed to use a calculator on all of the questions, but they will need to have any formulas already memorized.

The *Reading* section contains *40 questions* with four reading passages that must be completed within *35 minutes*. The passages are numbered, and your student will be asked questions about reading comprehension, literary devices, and terms.

The *Science* section of the tests contains *40 questions* and must be completed within *35 minutes*. This section has reading passages as well. It's important to note that this section of the ACT test will ask your student to pay attention to conflicting viewpoints. Test takers say that the Science section is more focused on critical skills than specific scientific knowledge.

The final section of the test is the *Essay*, and it's an optional part of the ACT. The essay is designed to assess how well your student can evaluate and analyze complex issues. They'll be asked to read a prompt and then write about their own perspective. There isn't a word count limit on this essay, but it has to be completed in the allotted *40 minutes*.

Your student will receive a composite score from the multiple-choice sections of the ACT test *and* also an essay score. For most colleges and universities, the essay score is the least important part of your student's ACT score. However, a really good performance on the essay can boost your child's overall score, which is something to keep in mind if they're a good writer.

Time and Strategy for the ACT

The ACT test takes *2 hours and 55 minutes* to complete. If your student chooses to take the essay portion of the test, that adds an additional 40 minutes. However, because of the time limitations on the ACT, it's really helpful for your student to manage their time well. They need to keep moving through the test, maintaining a steady pace so they don't get stuck on one question that keeps them from finishing the rest.

So how are the ACT questions scored? Each question in each section of the test is worth one point for a correct answer. Each of the four sections are then added together and averaged to get a composite score. The good thing about the composite score is that if your student is really good in English and reading but struggles in math, they can still pull out a good overall average on the ACT. The other thing to keep in mind about scoring is that there's no penalty for wrong answers. From a test-taking strategy standpoint, that means your student should never leave a question blank. They can't lose points for wrong or blank answers. Testing experts suggest you go through the timed section of each test and answer all of the questions you know in order to get those points. You never want to spend too much time on any one question.

Remember, when your student is taking the ACT, time is a key factor. If they simply skip the questions they don't know on the first pass-through of a section, they can go back when they're finished and try to eliminate any answer choices they know are incorrect. That will cut down on their chance of missing the question. For example, when your student gets through the science section, they can go back to a question they left unanswered. By re-reading the question and eliminating the obvious wrong answers, it leaves the better choices, and your kid can take their best guess with better odds of being right.

WHEN YOUR STUDENT IS TAKING THE ACT, TIME IS A KEY FACTOR.

If they run into a question and just have no idea which answer is correct, it's recommended that they choose one letter and fill in that same letter on all questions they don't know or can't eliminate options on. For example, your student would fill in the third option on every question they don't know. Remember, they have a 25 percent chance of being correct on each question, and this strategy actually improves your chance of winning the guessing game.

As we touched on previously, I strongly recommend

your student takes an ACT timed practice test. Repetition is valuable as you prepare—and so is getting used to the time crunch. I'd suggest that your student begin their prep by visiting the princetonreview.com site for more information. The ACT is currently offered seven times per year in September, October, December, February, April, June, and July. Registration is typically a month before the testing date. Your student is allowed to retake the ACT up to twelve times. I really encourage you to make a plan for your child to take the test multiple times. Hopefully that gives you a little more insight into the ACT. Now, let's take a closer look at the SAT.

A CLOSER LOOK INTO THE SAT

The SAT test was updated in 2016, so the test format is different from what you or one of your student's older siblings may have taken. The new format of the SAT is much closer to the ACT. The updated SAT test is now 45 minutes shorter, but it allows for longer periods of time to work on a single subject. The newer version of the test also has fewer questions and no penalty for choosing wrong answers. This allows for a testing strategy similar to the ACT. The new scoring range for the SAT is 400–1600, and the essay results are reported separately. The College Board also made some changes to the reading, math, and essay sections of the test.

The SAT is broken down into these major test sections: Evidence-Based Reading, Writing and Language, Math, and the optional Essay. Like the ACT, the questions are all multiple choice, and each offers four answers to choose from.

The first section is called the *Reading*, and it includes *52 questions* that must completed in *65 minutes*. This portion of the test has five major reading passages focused on literature, historical documents, social sciences, and natural sciences. The questions in this section are designed to assess if your student understands the information and the ideas in the reading.

The next section of the SAT is *Writing and Language*. It contains *44 questions* that must be completed in *35 minutes*. These questions are focused on your student's grammar, vocabulary, and editing knowledge and skills.

The *Math* section includes *58 questions* with a total of *80 minutes* to complete those questions. This section is broken up into four major areas with a 20-question, no-calculator section (with a 25-minute time limit) and a 38-question section where a calculator is allowed (with a 55-minute time limit). The specific areas covered in the Math section are algebra I and II, problem solving and data analysis, geometry, some trigonometry, and complex numbers.

Finally, the SAT also has an *Essay* section, and like the ACT, it's optional. The essay is designed to assess how well your student can comprehend source material, analyze an argument, and write effectively. Your child will read a passage and explain how the writer builds a persuasive argument in a *50-minute* time period.

Here are a few quick strategy pointers on the SAT's essay. The format of the essay doesn't ask for an opinion, so make sure your student doesn't use "I" or "you" in their writing response. Writing legibly can also help your child's scoring, and they should use an introductory paragraph with a clear thesis statement just like they learned in their high school English class.

Time and Scoring for the SAT

The total time allotted for the SAT is *3 hours* without the Essay portion. The essay adds 50 minutes to the total time. The scoring of the SAT test is a little more complex than the ACT simply because it uses a variety of equating processes. Basically, every correct answer in a test section is used to create the student's raw score. The raw score is distributed across the different test areas. There isn't a penalty for wrong answers on the test. So that means, from a strategy perspective, that your student should never leave any answers blank. You don't lose points for wrong or blank answers, but you only get points for correct answers.

This means the testing strategy for the SAT is now similar to the strategy for taking the ACT. Test takers can go through the section and answer all of the questions they know first in order to get those points. They should skip over questions they don't know the answer to. Then, they can go back to the questions they skipped and work to eliminate the multiple-choice answers they know are incorrect. If they can narrow it down to two options and then guess, their percentage of being correct goes up from 25 percent to 50 percent. Like the ACT strategy, in their final pass through the handful of questions they don't know, they should simply choose the same letter for all of them.

THE GOOD NEWS ABOUT THE SAT IS THAT STUDENTS HAVE MORE TIME TO COMPLETE EACH SECTION.

The good news about the SAT is that students generally have more time to complete each section. Your child will likely have the chance to go back and look through questions they were unsure of their first time through. The suggested preparation for the SAT is similar to the ACT. Unlike the ACT, though, there's no limit to how many times your student can take the SAT. The test is offered seven times a year just like the ACT, but the College Board only keeps record of your last six attempts. Your student can do additional research on how best to prepare at the princetonreview.com website.

It's important that your student develops and follows a study plan for these tests starting in the spring of sophomore year and continuing through the summer to those first official test dates in eleventh grade. Now, as we wrap up our discussion of the X's and O's of the ACT and SAT games, there is one more common test-related term we should talk about.

SUPERSCORING AND ITS BENEFITS

Ethan was a strong math student hoping to score high enough on his ACT to get a scholarship to a pre-med program at a big university in Texas. He told me that his first scores came back and his Math and Science sections were high, but his English and Reading were low and brought his overall score down. Ethan wasn't discouraged though. He had done his research and knew that the university he applied to accepted *superscoring*.

He went back and took the ACT two more times, preparing in advance for only one section at a time: first English, then Reading. After taking the test two more times, Ethan had solid scores in all four sections. The university accepted his top score in each area of all the tests, and his composite score was even higher than he anticipated. Ethan ended up with the scholarship he needed because of his work preparing for and taking the ACT. Superscoring can be a huge advantage for your teen, just like it was for Ethan, and it can change their approach to testing. So let's take a closer look at how it works.

Superscoring is when a college will accept your student's highest score in each section of the test—Math, English, Reading, and Science—from all of the testing attempts. Then they will use those high section scores in their formulation of your student's composite score. This can translate into more scholarship dollars but does mean that your student has to commit to taking the test multiple times. Superscoring is done for both the ACT and the SAT. Let's run through a quick example of how it works.

Say that your student takes the ACT and gets a 24 in English, a 28 in Math, a 26 in Reading, and a 23 in Science. The ACT adds those four scores and divides them by four to get a composite score of *25*.

If your student tests again and receives a 28 in English, 29 in Math, 29 in Reading, and 29 in Science, that would equal a composite score of *28*.

Then let's say on your student's third try they receive a 29 in English, 24 in Math, 29 in Reading, and a 29 in Science for a composite of *27*.

I know that's a lot of numbers, but it demonstrates this: if the school accepts the highest scores from each section, the results would be a 29 in English, a 29 in Math, a 29 in Reading, and a 29 in Science, for a composite score of *29*. That's one to four points higher than all the previous attempts, and it could translate to more scholarship money!

///

ALMOST 90 PERCENT OF COLLEGES WILL SUPERSCORE THE SAT AND 68 WILL SUPERSCORE THE ACT.

///

Now, almost 90 percent of colleges will superscore the SAT and 68 percent will superscore the ACT. Start by finding out if the colleges and universities on your student's list will superscore. If so, encourage your student to study really hard with a focus on one area of the test and just kill that section. Then take the test again focused on the next section, and so on, until you get the composite score you want. It will cost a little more up front to take the test multiple times, but it's definitely worth your time and investment.

LEAN IN

It's not uncommon for students and parents to feel overwhelmed by the big tests. A lot of folks end up looking like an ostrich with their head stuck in the sand when it's time to face them head-on. But remember that success is all about the proper, prior planning. I am telling you: this is doable. Re-read this chapter. Dig into the testing websites. The more you and your kid learn about the tests and the strategies to do well, the better and more empowered your teen will feel!

YOUR DEBT-FREE DEGREE PLAN

+ Discuss with your student the differences between the ACT and SAT and which test is a better fit for them.
+ Get as familiar as possible with the SAT and ACT tests.
+ Determine with your student how many times they will take a test and when they will start the process.
+ Ask your child to research test prep courses and bring you their top choices.
+ Make sure your student knows which tests their preferred colleges accept and if they superscore test results.
+ If you or your child is feeling overwhelmed, talk to other parents and students who have already walked down this road. Find out what worked for them and what tips or tricks they used.
+ Make sure your teenager is prepared physically for taking the big tests. They should get a good night's sleep the night before and eat a healthy breakfast the morning of the test.

8

JUNIOR YEAR: WELCOME TO THE MAIN EVENT

If you just picked up this book and started reading Chapter 8 first because your student is a junior, I'm so glad you've joined us! I was in a similar situation, just beginning to think about college late into my junior year in high school. If you're feeling panicked, I want you to take a deep breath. I've got your back. We're going to take the mystery out of the college process. I'm going to show you how to get your child to college without debt, even starting this year. Now, will you do me favor? Please go back and start reading at the Introduction. We've walked through a lot of important steps in the first seven chapters and you'll want to catch up. Choose the steps that apply to you and your student (many of them will), do them, and then catch back up with us here.

THE NEW NORM

I met Graham at a high school in Georgia after one of my talks. He came up to ask for some advice on how to pay for college. Honestly, he was pretty stressed out. He explained how he had hoped to get into a prestigious local tech university to study engineering, but even though his test scores were good, he hadn't qualified for enough scholarship money. He was well into his junior year and felt like if he didn't make it to this particular school, his long-term goals would be crushed and he'd never be able to succeed.

As we talked, it was evident Graham felt enormous anxiety and that those emotions were clouding his judgment. This young man had so much going for him. The truth was he was going to be successful no matter what college he went to. In fact, Graham said multiple schools were offering him better financial incentives that put a debt-free college education within his reach. He was a high achiever and he was locked into his goals, but his feelings were keeping him from seeing his position clearly.

Everything about going to college ramps up junior year, including the emotions your teen is going to feel. And just like feelings can cloud your judgment as a parent, those overwhelming feelings can prove to be hurdles for kids as well. Students like Graham are the norm. Make sure you're ready to coach your kid as they experience these big emotions. It's going to be all too easy for your student to look at a school that's out of reach financially and sign up for loans to cover their bills. The devastating consequences of taking on that debt may not even register with your student because they're laser focused on going to a particular school at all costs. *Your student needs you to be the voice of reason as they make this life-changing decision.* Take a minute with me to put yourself in your child's place and get a feel for all that they're feeling.

COLLEGE IS A HUGE CHANGE

Going to college is a *huge* deal. You're welcome.

Yes, I know that's another obvious statement, but really think about this for a moment. Your child has been under your wing for eighteen years. They've only known living under someone else's roof. They've had you looking out for them, helping them make good choices, for years. This is their very first big step on their own. It can be a serious emotional roller coaster for students. They're facing incredible pressure to perform. Your teen is being asked to:

+ focus on their grades and extracurricular activities,
+ do well on the ACT and SAT tests,
+ find enough scholarships to cover school, and
+ get out of your house!

And at every turn they're being asked by people they know as well as complete strangers what they want to be when they grow up. Only instead of the carefree answers that are expected from a young child, this time it's for real. The stakes have never been higher as they consider: *What do I want to do for the rest of my life? Where do I want to go to school? Where do I want to live? How am I going to come up with thousands of dollars to pay for this?*

And then there are the really scary questions underneath all of the other ones: *Can I even get into college? What happens if I don't get into my top choice school? What if I flunk out? What if I can't make new friends and handle being on my own for the first time? What happens if I fail?*

That's a whole lot of adult-sized weight sitting on your teenager's shoulders. Even writing this in my thirties, I can clearly remember the enormous pit in my stomach as I faced those same questions.

As adults, you and I have already walked through some intense fear and pressure in life. But in all likelihood, going to college without debt is the biggest, baddest mountain your child has ever had to climb. They are going to need you this year like never before. The stress is real. The pressure is real. Be prepared for these emotions and be ready to reassure them that everything will be okay—because as scary as this all may seem at times, it really will work out.

IT'S GO TIME

Junior year is go time. All of the preparation and activities up to this point have laid a solid foundation for success, and now it all shifts into high gear. In junior year, you want your student to narrow down their list of colleges. Start by pulling out that list and together look honestly at how those schools do or don't match up to your child's situation this year: things like their career goals, current and expected GPA, location, and what college savings is available, if any. Then choose the top three to five schools that are the best match for your teen.

If you haven't done so already, this is a great place to stop and ask your student what's important to them about each of those schools. Really dig in to understand why these three to five colleges appeal to your teen. Maybe ultimately, the appeal is more about prestige than being a wise financial choice for their future. Or maybe they're shortchanging themselves because they don't believe they can win any scholarships. This can be a good place to course correct their steps if needed.

Now, this list of top college choices should be realistic. I'm not saying they can't still have a far-reaching dream school on the list. What I'm saying is don't put all of your eggs in one basket. You want to have more than one school picked out because there are still a lot of factors to consider. Have an in-state option. Have a community college option. Then make sure you're very familiar with the admissions requirements *and* application deadlines for those schools—including early admission policies and deadlines.

Eleventh grade is also when your student's ACT or SAT scores officially count for college admissions. Have your student take their test prep course and practice tests. Test preparation courses aren't necessarily cheap, but they cost far less than full tuition and can lead to good scholarships. One student I know named Lizzie took the ACT and initially earned a 24. Then she took a reputable prep class and raised her ACT score to 27. This earned her an additional $12,000 in scholarships.

Keep in mind the actual ACT or SAT testing dates when you sign up for the prep class. Also, re-read Chapter 7 to make sure you and your child have planned out when and how many times they're going to take the big tests. Remember, they can take the ACT and SAT up to January of their senior year and still have their scores count toward college admission. This deadline varies, though, so be sure to check with the individual colleges your child is interested in.

A word of warning: testing can be extremely stressful for students. My friend Jennifer is a local educational psychologist and tells me she's seeing an increasing number of students under harmful pressure to score well. Students are feeling like their entire future is on the line, and if they don't score a 32 on the ACT or a 1300 on the SAT, they're going to be a failure. The effects are real and completely unnecessary.

If you suspect your kid is putting too much pressure on themselves, it's important to tell them that all you require on this test is that they do their best. Really, they can't do more than this. Jennifer recommends parents tell their kids, "Do your best and we will figure out the rest." Also, remind your teen that they can take the test multiple times. Their entire future isn't dependent on this one three-hour block of time this coming Saturday. This should help ease some test anxiety.

COLLEGE FAIRS

With all of the hard work to build a strong college resumé well under way, it's time to get some deeper exposure to colleges. A college fair can be really helpful as you consider the possibilities. Think of it like house hunting. Before you buy or rent a home, you want to get a feel for your options and discover what appeals to you. Do you like an urban setting or country living? Do you want a large house or a small one? College fairs can help your student learn what the possibilities are so they can make an informed decision.

When you're looking at colleges, it's not just what school has the best program for a specific career path. You want to factor in all aspects of a school and if it's a fit for your student: Is it located close to home or far away, is the school in a large city or a rural community, is it a huge school with tens of thousands of students or a smaller community with a few thousand? And even if the schools at the fair aren't necessarily on your student's list, these events are helpful because of the sheer number of colleges present. You and your student will likely learn some things you didn't know before. Your student might even discover a new college.

Bobby now attends a small private university in Georgia that he didn't even know existed until he attended a local college fair held by his school district and spoke with an admissions counselor. He's now enrolled on a full academic scholarship, studying in a great engineering program, and loves the small college-town atmosphere of the community.

COLLEGE VISITS

Once your student has their final college list narrowed down to three to five schools, it's time to plan college visits. I know it might sound early to do serious college visits as a junior in high school, but it's not. Your impression of a university can change in a big way once your feet hit campus. Your student needs these visits to rank their top colleges.

///

YOUR IMPRESSION OF A UNIVERSITY CAN CHANGE IN A BIG WAY ONCE YOUR FEET HIT CAMPUS.

///

A few housekeeping items up front. Encourage your student to find out when the university has official visits. Many schools do organized tours in the fall, but most also provide tours all year while students are on campus. I would *always* recommend going to see a school when the students are there.

Also, check with your teen's high school about their policies for college visits. Some school districts allocate a certain number of excused absences for those visits. This can be important if your student is involved in advanced placement classes that are difficult to miss. Joe, a junior at a local high school, was taking a full load of AP courses. He was only able to make up quizzes and tests in these courses if he was out with an excused absence. His school district's designated college days were critical to helping keep up his GPA.

If your student has younger siblings, let them tag along on these college visits and start dreaming about their own college adventure. My friend Jason and his wife, Stephanie, have six kids and when one is ready for a college tour, they take everyone along. It sounds kind of crazy, but he said it's made a big impact on how serious his younger kids are about college prep and planning!

THE ESSENTIAL COLLEGE VISIT CHECKLIST

As you and your student prepare to visit colleges, write down the goals you want to accomplish and the questions you want answered on your visits. Rea and her dad sat down together after they scheduled campus visits for her top three colleges and came up with a checklist of what she felt was important to discover on each campus. They wrote down a list of questions for the admissions counselors, the professors she was scheduled to meet, and for the student tour guides. Rea told me that the college trips with her dad went by in a blur of excitement and the questions really helped her focus critically on which school was the best fit for her.

Now, I know that many of the things you're going to look for on these campuses will be specific to your student and their interests. But there are also some "must-haves" you should make sure are on your list.

If you don't know them already, find out important

calendar dates while you're on campus: early admission, early application, work-study programs, early scholarship programs, and when FAFSA has to be done.

Also check with the admissions counselors to determine what's required of freshmen. I would ask if they have to live on campus their freshman year and if a meal plan is required—and, if so, what the minimum is. Also, are freshman students allowed to bring a car to campus? (There are many universities that won't allow first-year students to have a car.)

Be sure to try the food and visit the dorms or on-campus apartments. If possible, sit in on a class. If you're able to visit a class, be sure your student arrives early and introduces themselves to the professor. They should stay for the entire class, pay close attention, and refrain from taking pictures or videos. Also, be respectful of any guidelines the school has for class visits. Some ask that only students attend—not parents or siblings.

As you and your kid are planning college visits, ask in advance if they can meet one-on-one with a current student. Some schools will help set up a meeting between your child and a current student who is majoring in what your teen is interested in. Doing this will help your child get a better feel for the school. Students will usually be very honest with other students about their experience—more so than university employees or professors. Make sure to ask them about both what they like about the college and what they don't!

Also, don't neglect the opportunity to speak with a professor on your visit. Very few people do and it can be especially helpful. Again, you likely need to call ahead and make arrangements for this. If your student knows the program they want to pursue, call that department office and ask for an appointment to meet a professor or the department chair. Otherwise, just choose a subject your kid is interested in.

When you sit down with a professor, ask them how long they've taught at the school. Don't be afraid to ask them for their honest thoughts about their program and the university. And parents, pay special attention to how the professor interacts with your student. Are they taking your child's questions seriously? Are they engaged or distracted? Are they being helpful?

College visits are a good time to get clarity on costs for each school as well. The total cost of a school isn't always obvious from the brochures and websites. There's a lot more involved than just tuition: it's tuition *and* room and board *and* meal plans *and* fees *and* books *and* potentially Greek life, intramurals, and clubs! When my friend Mike took his daughter Brittany—a future math major—on college tours, she created a spreadsheet to compare the total costs of each school. When they returned, they had all of the comparative costs viewable side by side.

While you're adding up those costs, remember to add a line for hidden fees that have nothing to do with the school's costs. I remember seeing three entire aisles full of products for Target's back-to-school sale last summer. Parents, I know it may sound crazy, but this is a real thing. You need to factor in the cost of furnishing your student's dorm room. I talked with a parent whose daughter got a credit card and spent a little over $5,000 to furnish her *dorm room* with a recliner, posters, blankets, pillows, and a flat-screen television. The dad said that he didn't even drive a $5,000 *car* when he was eighteen years old!

Of course, you should never take on credit card debt for anything, especially to furnish a dorm room, so be sure to plan ahead and budget for the stuff your kid needs. There will also be a fee for campus parking. And then you'll need to factor in the cost of normal, everyday life stuff like: doing laundry, going out to eat, sporting events, and most important, the cost of driving or flying home! All of this adds up.

One last thing: while you're on these college visits, you're going to hear the words *financial aid* thrown around a bunch. Keep in mind it usually includes a variety of things: grants, work-study, scholarships, and loans. When the time comes to review financial aid packages, you'll need to look closely at what the school is offering your child. Certain types of financial aid, like scholarships and work-study, are helpful. But avoid student loans at all cost.

As you wrap up your college visits, gather up all your notes and reflect with your student on your experiences. Talk about what they saw on the visits, how they felt about the campuses, the towns, the distances from home, the students and professors, and of course, the food! Talk about any significant observations you had. Compare the costs of each school with them. Make it fun! Remember, you and your child only get to go through this process once, and you're teaching them the process for how to make good life choices.

YOUR DEBT-FREE DEGREE PLAN

+ If you're just picking up this book as the parent of a junior and you started reading this chapter first, please go back and start reading at the Introduction. Otherwise, you'll miss some steps that will make this process a positive experience for you and your child.

+ Put yourself in your teenager's shoes for a few minutes. Look at the world through their eyes and with their experiences. Reflect on what it's like to be them as a junior in high school. Let this perspective help you as you coach them through this process.

+ Encourage your student to narrow down their list of college choices to three to five. Make sure they're a good fit for your child and their goals.

+ Consider if you and your teen should attend a college fair.

+ If you haven't already, make sure your student takes a test prep course and does at least one practice ACT or SAT test.

+ Ask your teen to schedule and begin taking either the ACT or SAT test. Plan on them taking the test multiple times.

+ Take some pressure off your student as they face the big tests by reminding them to do their best and you'll figure out the rest together.

+ Work together with your teen to schedule their college visits and attend them. Write down goals for each visit as well as questions for the people you'll meet. Make sure they ask to meet with a professor and current student in advance. Also, check out my website anthonyoneal.com for my "Essential College Visit Checklist" for your student. It shows them what they need to know, do, and ask as they prepare for each of their college visits.

+ Be thorough in researching all the costs for your student to attend college—even things like decorating a dorm room and traveling home for the holidays.

9

SENIOR YEAR: THE HOME STRETCH

This is it! Your student's senior year—the home stretch to high school graduation and the beginning of a new adventure.

For any parents of seniors joining us for the first time in Chapter 9, welcome! We're going to help you figure out where to start and the steps to take to get your student through college debt-free. I want you to know right here, right now that *this is possible*. If you're just starting the journey with a senior in high school, your choices may be more limited than if you'd started earlier—you may have to be more creative than others—but your child really can get a college degree without taking on student loans.

I know this may feel a bit backward, but I need you to go back and start reading from the Introduction. The Introduction through Chapter 8 contain a lot of valuable information you and your teen are going to need. (Don't worry! I wrote this to be a quick read on purpose. It won't take you that long.) Take the information that's helpful and applicable to your student, do those steps, then meet back up with me here.

FINISH STRONG!

I want to tell you about Chad's experience in the fall of his senior year in high school. His parents shared with me that he was focused and on track. He had a 4.0 GPA and enough scholarships and grants already to cover his preferred in-state college choice *completely*. He either had or was currently taking the rest of the credits he needed to graduate from high school and was able to focus on a dual enrollment class to help knock out some college credit. But Chad ended up making some poor choices early in his senior year.

He had an elective film class that he didn't take seriously and he missed the end-of-the-quarter exam and received an F. He also chose to take part in a school tradition of doing a senior prank the night before homecoming. He played a small role in a large group of seniors sneaking some farm animals onto the locked football field the night before the game. While the prank seemed harmless enough, it resulted in property damage and the seniors got into trouble with local law enforcement. All fun and games, right? Nope. Because of those two choices, Chad's parents said he lost several merit scholarships and was forced to change his college plans and attend community college for his freshman year.

Now, I know Chad's story is kind of a bummer. But it's not uncommon for seniors to make silly decisions as high school winds down. The message we want to communicate to them is that *senior year matters*. The number one challenge I throw down when I'm speaking to high school seniors is that they need to focus on finishing strong.

ONE OR TWO UNWISE DECISIONS CAN UNDO YEARS OF HARD WORK.

I'm sure you've heard of senioritis—the "disease" where your student really slacks off and stops taking school and their commitments seriously. It can be a real challenge for some teens and, like Chad discovered, it's costly. One or two unwise decisions can undo years of hard work. While colleges mainly look at a student's GPA from the ninth to eleventh grades, it's still important to keep that average up the last year of school. More and more colleges are checking into what's happened during a student's last year of school. And there are a number of cases of students losing scholarships or grants because they didn't keep their grades up. Finishing strong means staying engaged through both semesters of senior year. There are several ways you can help your student do this.

First, as your child chooses their classes for senior year, talk to them about taking a math class. Taking a fourth math class in high school confirms to college admissions counselors that your teen can handle academic rigor. There's also research that reflects a higher level of college success for students who take math in high school all four years. In one study, 26 percent of students who took only three years of high school math required some remediation once they got to college. But only 17 percent of students who did four years of high school math needed help in college.[41]

Another way to help your teen stay focused is for them to take dual enrollment courses. This can actually be pretty fun for students. They'll be getting college credits at a fraction of the cost, which is super helpful. But they'll also be in a different learning atmosphere taught by college professors and, potentially, even hosted at a local community college. This kind of environment can be very encouraging to students.

I know a student named Jenny who was honestly just

ready to be done with high school her senior year. She was mature for her age and was tired of the classroom drama. Jenny took a history class at her local community college one day a week as part of the dual enrollment program through her high school. Every Tuesday afternoon she got to leave school early, drive over to the community college, and walk around campus. She got to see how college students interacted with one another and participated in class. She got to hear lectures and answer questions from a college professor and read more advanced books. It was all new, and she loved every single minute of it. She told me that this history class kept her motivated in her other classes because it was a glimpse of what college would be like. Now she wanted to go more than ever.

Parents, think through ways you can encourage your student to stay focused and finish strong this year. Maybe it's visiting their college of choice. Maybe it's meeting new professionals already doing what they want to do. Maybe it's taking a weekend seminar. Your student will probably really appreciate your help as they finish out their time in high school.

SENIOR YEAR CHECKLIST

During this final push to college there will be a lot of things fighting for your kid's time and attention. As much as possible, keep the focus senior year on finding scholarships. This is absolutely critical to going to college without debt. Ask your student to commit to hunting for scholarships an hour every day—whether during study hall or at home in the evenings—and encourage them to pay close attention to the deadlines.

Your senior may still need to take the ACT or SAT, either for the first time if you're just now starting the college process or as part of your strategy to raise their test scores for admissions or scholarships. While dates vary by school, if your child is applying for early admissions, the November of their twelfth grade year is likely the latest date your student's score can be used for college admissions. If they're applying for regular admission, some schools accept test scores as late as January of senior year. Make sure they schedule their test accordingly.

By senior year some students have lost track of the volunteer hours they need in order to graduate. If that's your student, make sure they complete any necessary hours by the end of their first semester senior year. Also, if there are any questions about your student's readiness for graduation, have them meet with their guidance counselor as soon as possible.

There are usually some students who are still checking out colleges at the beginning of their senior year of high school. This is totally okay. Just make sure you and your child understand that the clock is ticking. They should schedule college visits as early in the school calendar as possible. It's also important to realize their chance of acceptance is going to start dropping because colleges are filling up with early admission candidates.

STAY ON TOP OF THOSE DEADLINES!

Your student will be making important college decisions senior year. This can be everything from deciding on what college to attend to what dorm they want to live in. Your teen should pay close attention to the calendar and stay on top of all deadlines and correspondence from colleges. You don't want your teen to miss out on a great opportunity because of disorganization.

Being on top of the deadlines impacts more than just college admissions and scholarship opportunities. It can make a difference in your student's freshman year of college. I talked with a college freshman named Marie who told me early admission enabled her to take advantage of her excellent high school GPA and get into the honors program at her university. It also allowed her to move into one of the best dorms on campus (reserved for honor students). And because she took care of business early, she was also able to find a roommate who was already in the honors program.

If she hadn't completed the process early, none of those options would have been available to her. A good deal of college housing is first come, first serve and the same holds true for academic programs that can benefit your student. Pay close attention to all deadlines. If your student is unsure of what they are, make sure they ask. Some students have found it helpful to keep a master list of all college and scholarship websites, usernames, passwords, and deadlines. It's easy to create and a simple way to track all of the details in one place.

TO EARLY ADMIT OR NOT

If your student knows exactly where they want to go, consider if they should apply for early admissions. About 450 colleges offer early admission plans according to the College Board.[42] Early admission is when a student applies earlier than usual to college and finds out if they're admitted early too. Applications are generally due in October or November of senior year. Admissions decisions are often made in December or January of senior year. Your FAFSA form can be submitted starting October 1.[43]

Now, what can be a little tricky is that there are several types of early admission plans. Some are binding. These are usually called *early decision plans*. For this plan, your student can only apply early to one school, and if the college accepts you and offers enough financial aid, you must attend that school. Other plans are not binding. These are usually called *early action plans*. Your student can apply to more than one school in this scenario and, if accepted, may decline to attend.

Early admission is helpful for some students but not all students. For some, it can help them get into their first-choice school. But others may want more time to show colleges what classes and grades they're capable of or to find out what kind of scholarships they will receive. If your senior has a first-choice school in mind, it's a good idea to check with the admissions office to find out when most students are actually accepted. That'll give you a good idea of when your kid should submit their paperwork. Normal admissions for most schools begins in March and must be completed no later than May of senior year.

THE BENEFITS OF CLEP TESTING

Another option to explore senior year is CLEP testing. CLEP stands for College Level Examination Program, and it's a series of tests sponsored by the College Board. There are currently thirty-three different tests offered on a wide range of subjects. These are credit-by-examination tests. If your student passes the exam, they will earn college credit for a one-semester class. This obviously translates to cost savings on tuition and shortens the time you need to earn your degree.

Now, your student will need to find out what their preferred schools accept in the way of CLEP testing. (Every school is different.) Tests usually cost around $100 to take, but there is a program that will help your student take the test for free. Check out the College Board website for more information about that.[44]

CLEP tests usually take between 90 and 120 minutes to complete. They're administered at testing centers and are computer-based, multiple-choice style tests. Practice tests are available online and study guides are available for purchase to prepare for each test. You can find the subjects online at the College Board website. Like dual enrollment courses, this is another low-cost way to get a smart start on the next phase of your student's academic journey.

WRAP UP THE HEAVY LIFTING

Senior year is when your student is going to make the big decision: where they're going to school. If your student has applied for early admission, most of the college decisions should be locked in by December of senior year. If they've applied for regular admission, they usually have until May 1 to make their final decision.

So how do you help your student decide which school is best? It's actually pretty fun to watch this process unfold. Of course, you're going to look realistically at the following:

+ Where have they been accepted?
+ Which program is best suited for their career goals?

+ Which school appeals to them most?
+ Which school (or schools!) makes the most sense financially?

As you weigh all the factors involved, one college will naturally rise to the top. It may actually surprise you which one, but you'll know and it will be a big moment for you and your child.

You may have an experience like my colleague Sharon. Her son wanted so badly to go to a top university in a different state. He had worked his tail off in high school, but when he and his parents started reviewing what scholarships had come in, he realized he didn't have enough to pay cash for it. He was devastated for a while but realized what he had to do. His dad worked for a well-known private university in town. Because of that, he could go there for free. Did he want to go to college where his dad worked? No, he wanted to do something on his own. But will he get an outstanding education and graduate without debt? *Yes!*

If your teen is still looking at colleges in December of senior year, you may have an uphill climb in front of you. I would recommend you check out community college options for that first year, as colleges can fill up quickly. As we've discussed throughout the book, there are many benefits in taking the two-year college approach, including spending far less on prerequisite classes.

IF YOUR KID IS A SENIOR AND
YOU'RE SHORT ON CASH

Given the cost of a college education, it's not unusual to find yourself the parent of a senior who doesn't have enough cash to pay for school. If that's you, there are two really great community college options to consider.

First, like we've talked about previously, your student can do their first two years of school at your local community college—taking general education classes—while living at home and working as much as possible. This will help them get their grades up, if needed, and give them time to prepare for the big tests and to research careers and four-year schools. (Yes, they still need to do all of that prep work.) They need to save every dime they make and relentlessly hunt for scholarships. Their sophomore year in college, they can apply to a four-year school—usually an in-state school—and transfer starting their junior year, using scholarships and cash to pay for their last two years.

The second option is for your senior to use a free or low-cost community college to earn their associate's degree. Community colleges usually offer different tracks: one track to use if you want to transfer to a four-year school and other tracks that move you directly into the job market. After two years of earning their associate's degree, your student can apply for a full-time position with a company who will pay for them to finish their bachelor's degree. Many companies offer something like this, and it's a good option for students who cannot cash flow college.

I have a friend who works as an administrative assistant for an organization with a tuition reimbursement program. Every semester she takes one night-class and is on track to complete her bachelor's degree in six years. Now, if your student can work full time and take two classes each semester as well as a class or two during summer, they can finish their degree in less than six years. This process obviously takes longer than the typical four-year college plan, but the goal here is a debt-free education—not to beat a clock.

Deciding on a Major

As your student looks to college and their future career, they don't have to know yet what they want to major in—though it does help if they have some ideas about it. Most college students don't get close to coursework in their major until the second semester of their sophomore year. The truth is, if your student is engaged in their studies, they're going to grow leaps and bounds in that first year of school. As students gain experience, they usually have more clarity on what direction to go. If your student has absolutely no idea what they want to do, invest in some specialized career assessments. There are a lot of great options available today that will help them better understand themselves and what they're good at.

Ultimately, you want your student to choose a major

that balances passion and common sense. One of my colleagues, Rachel Cruze, laughs when she warns against students earning a four-year degree in left-handed puppetry, but parents, we are really serious about this. It does not make sense for your student to spend thousands of dollars earning a degree that isn't useful in the real world. Yes, we want them to do what they love, but we also want them to be able to pay their bills. They can pursue their passion but also be wise in how they pursue it.

IT DOES NOT MAKE SENSE FOR YOUR STUDENT TO SPEND THOUSANDS OF DOLLARS EARNING A DEGREE THAT ISN'T USEFUL IN THE REAL WORLD.

DOES YOUR STUDENT NEED A GAP YEAR?

Senior year is also the best time to talk about a gap year. A *gap year*, sometimes called a "bridge year," is when a student takes a year off between high school graduation and the first year of college. Now, I do not recommend this for everyone, but it can make a big difference for some students. Maybe your senior is really excited about going to college, but very undecided about what to study. Maybe the finances aren't in order yet to pay for college. Your child could use a gap year to improve their ACT and SAT scores and raise the amount of scholarship money available to them. (If they choose to do this, be sure to pay attention to the testing, admissions, and scholarship deadlines just like during senior year.) And sometimes it's just good to allow kids an extra year to mature before they head off to school. I've met some sharp students who spent a year working, exploring their interests, volunteering, and basically growing up a little before they headed to college.

Jason spent his gap year volunteering at a homeless mission in Los Angeles. That year of service completely transformed him as a person and even changed the direction he wanted to go in college. When Jason drove to Los Angeles to work at the mission, he was set on pursuing a degree in logistics. That year made it obvious to him that he wanted to dedicate his life to serving the less fortunate. After seeing firsthand some of the fundraising challenges the mission faced, he decided to study accounting so he could focus on helping nonprofit ministries effectively manage their finances.

If a gap year is something your student thinks they want to pursue, you should know that many colleges accept their admission paperwork and allow them to defer for one year. In fact, there are some schools that host their own gap-year programs—usually service-learning programs—and some even offer funding for it.

You'll also want your student to check on any scholarships or grants they received to make sure the gap year doesn't disqualify them. Most athletes, for example, go directly to college so they don't lose their spot on the team and any athletic scholarship they received. At the end of the day, you don't want your student to lose free money for school. However, there are a growing number of experts who suggest that students who take a gap year arrive at college far more prepared to succeed than those who don't.[45]

FINAL THINGS

A lot of students and parents tell me that the second semester of their senior year feels way more like coming down the big hill of a roller coaster than they expected. Life may seem like it's moving really, really fast. But in these last few months before your child leaves home (if they're moving away for college) or gets really busy with community college and working, invest in some one-on-one time with them. My friend Luke took his daughter to an early breakfast every Thursday morning her senior year of high school to talk about her future and the things that really matter. Parents, soak in every minute right along with your child and be as intentional as possible as senior year wraps up.

YOUR DEBT-FREE DEGREE PLAN

+ Look for ways to help your student stay engaged their senior year and remind them of the importance of making sound decisions.

+ Encourage them to power through any feelings of senioritis.

+ Your student's main focus this year is to apply for as many scholarships as possible.

+ Your student should be wrapping up their ACT and SAT testing during fall semester, if not before.

+ Make sure your student has completed any volunteer hours, if required.

+ Encourage your student to stay on top of all deadlines and correspondence from colleges.

+ Think through if early admission is right for your student.

+ Consider if your student should take one or more CLEP tests for college credit as well as if a gap year would be beneficial.

+ Coach your student about how to choose their major.

+ Invest in spending time with your student.

+ Help your student decide which college to attend! Make sure it's the right fit for them and that all of the funding—scholarships, grants, and cash—is in place. If the funding isn't in place, either delay a year or choose a different option.

10

HOW TO BE SUCCESSFUL IN COLLEGE

Mom and Dad, you did it! I hope you cheered really loudly as your student walked across that stage! They've shown grit and determination and a lot of class. They've worked *hard* . . . and so have you. Take some time to really celebrate their wins and who they have become. Have a big dinner. Throw a party. Take a graduation trip. Whatever fits your family and your budget.

Once you come down off the graduation high, let's talk about one last thing: how to help your student be successful in college. Traveling the country to speak on college campuses, I get the chance to hear from hundreds of college freshmen about some of the struggles that they face, especially in that first year of school. Freshman year is a time of incredible growth, but it's also a year of starting over, establishing a new reputation, and learning what it means to be an adult. There is a lot of freedom and opportunity that can lead to great achievements or big downfalls.

My college story is actually one of the main reasons I am so passionate about teaching young people how to take ownership of their future. It's so easy for students to lose focus on what matters and make poor decisions that change everything. I know it was for me.

Let me give it to you straight: I, Anthony ONeal, got kicked out of college. That's right. And I'm telling you, it can happen to *any* young person who loses sight of their plan. As a freshman in college, I got really involved in Greek life. I made a lot of friends and had a blast. Of course, that was part of the problem. I was having way too much of a good time. I wasn't taking care of my business. And while I was busy making new friends and not applying myself, I was also introduced to those nice folks at the tables outside the cafeteria who worked for the credit card companies. They were handing out free pizzas, T-shirts, and future credit card debt! I ate the pizzas. I took the free T-shirts. And I think I filled out *all* the credit card applications. No joke.

Within two years, I had gotten kicked out of school and racked up $10,000 in student loan debt and $25,000 in other debt. I went from being a future-college-graduate to sleeping in my car in a Walmart parking lot. I had totally messed up my life. It was the lowest low.

Sadly, I run into young people all too often who have made the same mistakes. I met a sharp young lady who told me about her own poor choices in college. She'd worked really hard through high school to have the kind of GPA and test scores that earned her an academic full ride to an exclusive private university. It was an incredible situation. She rushed a sorority, got heavily involved in Greek life, and made a ton of really great friends. But her social choices started to impact her studies. Her freshman year ended up being too much of a party.

By the end of her first year, her grades were so low the college took away her full-ride scholarship. She had to move home, get a job, and enroll in a local college that she could pay for as she worked. Her poor choices changed everything.

Now, you may be thinking right now *My kid would never!* or *My kid ain't tryin' to be stupid like that!* I know, but the lesson I want to drive home is that it only takes one poor choice to undo all the incredible work your child has put in over these past few years.

FINAL WORDS

I've thought a lot over the years about what I wish I had done differently as a student. And I've thought a lot about what might have helped me make better choices. Some of that is in my other book written specifically for students headed to college, *The Graduate Survival Guide*. The rest I've put in this chapter for you parents. My life would have looked radically different if I had followed this wisdom. As moving day approaches and you start packing up your child's favorite books, their bedding, and all those shoes, I want to share with you the top ten things I wish I would have listened to as I started college. My guess is they will help your graduate too.

1. HAVE FUN (BUT DON'T BE STUPID)!

College is supposed to be a lot of fun! We want our students to really enjoy these four years: Play an intramural sport. Take a last-minute road trip to a different state. Participate in the funny (and legal and safe) freshman traditions on campus. Watch those hilarious movie marathons. Rush a fraternity or sorority. Join the late-night cramming sessions at the all-night diner. Take a crazy awesome spring break trip with friends. As long as your student keeps their priorities in check, encourage them to take full advantage of all that campus life has to offer.

As I look back at my time on campus, I wish someone had tapped me on the shoulder and reminded me of Jim Rohn's principle that we are the average of the five people we spend the most time with. Yes, we want them to enjoy campus life, but there are friends who work hard *and* play hard, and then there are friends who only play hard. Encourage your student to spend their time with people who are focused on both.

If your kid is frustrated by their roommate or the people they first meet, tell them to keep looking. It can take some time to find your tribe. They are looking for friends who will encourage them to be better in every way—and who will love them enough to say something if they're falling short.

2. KEEP YOUR FINANCIAL HOUSE IN ORDER.

I seriously cannot say this enough. This is an incredibly painful lesson to have to learn the hard way. Your student is setting the foundation for their future right now with their financial decisions: credit cards, student loans, spending habits, saving habits, giving habits. It's all very real now. With one signature they can make a mistake that will haunt them for decades.

YOUR STUDENT IS SETTING THE
FOUNDATION FOR THEIR FUTURE RIGHT
NOW WITH THEIR FINANCIAL DECISIONS.

Listen, we've talked about my debt. I was an 18-year-old kid who, in the blink of an eye, made the worst possible money decisions. Your student is going to be out on their own for the first time. Don't just assume they'll make good choices. Teach them how to do this right. Show them the budget breakdown in Chapter 1 of a recent college graduate with debt. The numbers don't lie! Help them write down a budget on paper if they're old school or get them started on the EveryDollar app they can download for free. Then check up on them monthly. Ask them how it's going, what's easy, where are they struggling. Continue to remind them of the freedom of debt-free living. And one more thing: remind them to keep hunting for scholarships. There is still money to be found for college expenses.

3. TREAT COLLEGE LIKE IT'S A JOB!

What does this mean? Well, for starters, it means to show up on time to everything—classes, events, study groups, meetings, lunches. Ultimately, this is a sign of respect for others as well as yourself.

It also means looking at the school day like a typical day at the office. That means from 8 in the morning until 5 in the afternoon, your student is either in class or studying for class. We're not taking afternoon naps like we did in kindergarten. We're not playing video games with roommates. We're working, and we're focused.

Treating college like a job means that students are conducting themselves professionally. It means they dress and behave appropriately. It means they respond to communication in a timely manner. They follow through with their commitments and deliver what's expected of them.

And parents, this is for you: if you're contributing to your student's college expenses, you need to make your expectations for them crystal clear. A lot of parents who help pay for their child's education tell their kids they expect them to go to class, to make good grades, and to graduate in four years. If they fail to meet these expectations, there are consequences (just like in the real world): they're coming home, and they're not getting any additional financial assistance for school. Whatever your expectations are, make sure you talk about them with your student ahead of time.

4. KEEP YOUR SOCIAL PRESENCE CLEAN.

There's a lot of silly stuff that happens on a college campus. A lot of it is harmless fun, but it has *no business* being posted on your student's social media. Emphasize again the importance of your child managing their personal brand. It won't be long before employers and HR professionals will be evaluating their online history to make hiring decisions. Remind them to keep it positive and professional. Also, have them consider starting a professional account on LinkedIn. They can start building their connections now: professors, peers, and people they meet in the community and at church.

5. GET TO KNOW THE PROFESSORS!

One of the greatest resources on a college campus is its college professors. Encourage your student to build strong relationships with them, just as they did with their high school teachers and counselors. Professors are obviously helpful with questions about class material, but their expertise doesn't end there. They can also help with networking, providing references, and offering support to students as they navigate life. If your student is nervous about approaching a professor, suggest they write down their questions in advance to help them remember what to say.

It's also important to help your student know how to choose their professors. Professors can make or break your experience with a subject. They can also be incredibly encouraging and sometimes discouraging too. Remember that colleges and universities hire professors because they are experts in their field, not necessarily because they're great teachers. When possible, students want to choose their classes by who the professor is, not based on time of day.

A young man named Seth had put off taking a

required American history class until his senior year in college. History had never been a favorite subject for him but that completely changed when he took this course. Instead of focusing only on memorizing dry names and dates, Seth's professor shared her passion for history through the stories of the actual people involved. For the first time, past events came alive for Seth. She also taught American history starting on the west coast and moving eastward rather than starting on the east coast and moving west. It made all the difference in the world, and Seth was hooked. It became one of his favorite classes in all four years of college.

Encourage your student to choose professors who know their subject matter, are invested in teaching well, and are interested in their student's success. If your student doesn't know who to choose, suggest that they talk to older students (who they trust) who have taken similar classes. Students will readily share their recommendations with one another.

6. FIND THE LIBRARY ON CAMPUS EARLY AND VISIT OFTEN.

In other words, study habits really matter. I wish someone had hit me upside the head and told me that part of the fun of college is the *opportunity to learn*. There are a whole lot of people in the world who don't get the luxury of studying great ideas and thinkers for four years. It's a really unique environment. Encourage them to take full advantage of this time by being curious and disciplined about their learning.

Also, let your student know that it's okay if they struggle academically (or at all). College is harder than high school. The same study habits that got your child into college may not get them through college. I heard a Harvard student talk about how he was at the top of his class in high school but barely made a C average in college. This was a really smart kid and even he had trouble! Regardless of where your child goes to college, they may have to do more, study differently, and ask for help frequently.

7. CHOOSE A DEGREE THAT WILL HELP YOU LAND A JOB.

I know this can sound anticlimactic after we've talked about students pursuing their passions, but hear me out. If your student gets to the end of their sophomore year in college and still has no idea what to major in—which can happen—guide them to a degree that will serve them regardless of the industry they wind up in. For example, a more general degree in business, management, marketing, or communications will give them a solid foundation in a lot of different types of companies. Just help them think through which general degree is most interesting to them.

Sometimes students also need to hear that choosing a major isn't going to forever define their future. Kids can put a lot of pressure on themselves to pick the perfect major. But the marketplace is full of folks who majored in one thing and their path led them to something entirely different. How many people do you know who now work in a field very different from their college major? I have one coworker who majored in journalism and spent over two decades in the military. He officially retired from the military, went back to school and got his master's degree in business (paying cash), and now works for one of our company's hardest-driving teams. A student's college major isn't final or fatal. It's just a stepping-stone in their journey.

CHOOSING A MAJOR ISN'T GOING TO FOREVER DEFINE YOUR CHILD'S FUTURE.

8. NEVER GIVE UP.

Expect bad days. We all have them. Your student will too. Maybe they answer a question in class incorrectly and feel foolish. Maybe they're embarrassed because they failed a big test. Maybe the guy or girl they're interested in doesn't show any interest in them. Maybe they're really struggling with their classes and don't want anyone to know. Maybe they're homesick—especially freshman year.

Let your student know now that bad days will happen. This isn't to rain on their parade but to prepare them so the bad days don't take them by surprise. When one hits, they can identify it. They know not to take it too seriously or to beat themselves up. Bad days happen. We learn from them and then get a fresh start tomorrow. The important thing is to never give up.

Parents, you might also want to learn a little about the resources available at your student's school before they get to campus. I'm talking about resources like academic and writing tutors, where to go if your child needs a doctor, the counseling office and what they specialize in, and the student life and housing offices. Then, if your student calls upset one day, you have an idea of where to point them.

9. REMEMBER YOUR *WHY.*

College life is full of (fun) distractions. Should I study for this test or go out to dinner and a movie with friends? Should I spend time hanging out tonight or get a reasonable amount of sleep? Should I eat those vegetables or an entire pizza and three cupcakes? Going to college means having more freedom in every area of life than ever before. Knowing and staying focused on your *why* is the secret to success.

I love the story about the guy who made a poster with the letter V and put it up in his dorm room freshman year. Each year, he moved that sign with him to his new dorm and kept it in a prominent spot in his room. People would sometimes ask him about it and he never would explain what it was about. His senior year, its meaning became obvious when he was named the valedictorian of his graduating class. He kept his *why* before him every single day.

For years, your student's *why* has been to get to college. Now that they're in college, they have to find their new *why*. Encourage your student to figure it out, write it down, and then keep it somewhere they can see every day. Focus and intentionality is everything, especially in college. Every single decision your student makes, even the fun ones, is serious.

10. TEND TO YOUR INNER WORLD.

We've talked pretty exclusively in this book about your child's outer world: classes, grades, extracurriculars, college resumés, future careers. But all of the success in the world is ultimately empty and meaningless because it doesn't create peace. American philosopher Dallas Willard said, "What matters is not the accomplishments you achieve; what matters is the person you become."[46] There's no question we want our children to be successful. We want them to achieve their goals and change the world. But what's more important than any of those great things is *who they become.*

As your child steps into adulthood, encourage them to pay attention to their inner world, not just their external one. Now, I am a Christian. I believe in talking and listening to God and walking according to his ways. For me, *becoming* means that things like love, joy, peace, patience, kindness, goodness, and self-control are increasing in my life. But even if you don't believe in God, tending to your inner world is still really important. Are you becoming a better person? Are you becoming more emotionally healthy? Either way, *becoming* doesn't happen by accident.

Parents, this is true for you and me too. A big transition like this can open up space to look again at who you're becoming. If you haven't thought about your own inner world in a while, there's nothing like a monumental life change to get you kick-started.

CONCLUSION

Okay, parents. Let's review. How do you send your kid to college without taking on debt?

You go to a school you can afford.

It's the same behavior, the same discipline, as every other aspect of your financial world. You take the emotion out of the decision. When you need a pair of shoes, you buy a pair that fits your budget. Sometimes that means your sneakers come from a garage sale. Sometimes it means a brand-name pair that costs hundreds of dollars. When you need a car, you buy one that fits your budget. Depending on your situation, that can be a $2,000 beater or it can be paying cash for a newer luxury car. The same is true for what college your student attends.

Think about how you would choose a college if it's strictly a business decision. In business we look for ROI, or our return on investment. It's basically the way we measure if something is a good idea. So for the ROI on where to attend college we would ask, "If College A costs five times more than College B, is my student going to get an education that's five times better at College A? Will my student make five times more on their annual salary if they attend College A?" If not, College A is probably not the best choice. You go to a school that makes sense.

Now, some people are going to tell you it does matter where you go to college. Some people are going to say that an expensive, elite school is *the key* to setting your child up for success. But the reality is that the name on a piece of paper will not make your child successful. Only your child can do that. A study from 2018 analyzed the CEOs of all the Fortune 500 companies and discovered that only 9.2 percent went to Ivy League schools.[47] Your kid may not get a particular job at a particular law firm in a particular city without a prestigious name on their diploma, but that doesn't mean they won't beat those same attorneys in court where it counts. *Your child is in control of their success.*

For most companies, what matters is that job applicants have a degree. It doesn't matter where their degree is from. Just this year alone at Ramsey Solutions our goal is to hire 300 new team members. That's a lot of people! You know how often we decline a candidate because they went to community college? Never. Dave Ramsey himself would tell you he doesn't even know where many of his folks went to school. It doesn't matter to him. What matters is a person's attitude and their results.

//

WHAT MATTERS IS THAT YOUR CHILD HAS A DEGREE. IT DOESN'T MATTER WHERE THEIR DEGREE IS FROM.

//

Parents, a college degree is a good thing! What's not a good thing is your kid being chained by debt for decades. Think for a minute about what happens when your child graduates from college debt-free. They can take most any job they want because they don't have a huge pile of debt to clean up. They can start saving money on their very first paycheck! They are beginning life way ahead of 70 percent of their peers.

Sending your kid to college without debt is nothing short of life-changing.

This is how you change your family tree.

DEBT-FREE DEGREE PLANNING

Alright now, parents, let's get started. Use these pages to track the progress you and your student make as you work toward getting to college debt-free. You can use these pages to dream together, set career goals, and record important information like GPAs, ACT and SAT scores, or college application deadlines. *You can do this!*

Get Real: Count the cost.

How much can you contribute to your child's education? Through part-time work or scholarships, how much can your child contribute? Use this space to crunch the numbers and get a realistic start on how much money is *really* on the table so you'll know how much *more* is needed. It takes proper, prior planning to avoid student loans!

Middle School: Start dreaming.

During your college/career chats, what have you discovered about your teen's dreams? Interests? Skills? College preferences? Career goals? Use this space to write them down, and don't forget to include a date. These are sure to change a bit over the years.

High School: Keep Track.

GPAs and ACT/SAT scores matter. You can use the chart below to record your student's progress. If your kid gets college credit from AP classes or dual enrollment, use this space to keep track of it. And don't forget those extracurricular activities. Anything worth including on a college application can be saved here.

SCORES					
	GPA	ACT	SAT	COLLEGE CREDITS EARNED	HONORS RECEIVED
Freshman					
Sophomore					
Junior					
Senior					

VOLUNTEERING			
	HOURS	ORGANIZATIONS SERVED	REFERENCES / CONTACTS
Freshman			
Sophomore			
Junior			
Senior			

EXTRACURRICULAR ACTIVITIES	
Freshman	
Sophomore	
Junior	
Senior	

College Visits: Compare Schools.

If you plan to visit more than one college campus, remembering *which* school had *what* may be difficult later. Use this space to jot down the specifics during each visit so you can quickly reference your likes and dislikes of each college.

COLLEGE:
DATE VISITED:
Questions:
Notes:

COLLEGE:
DATE VISITED:
Questions:
Notes:

COLLEGE:

DATE VISITED:

Questions:

Notes:

Applications: Get in.

APPLYING FOR COLLEGE				
SCHOOL	APPLICATION DUE DATE	REQUIREMENTS	APPLICATION SENT	ADMISSIONS CONTACT INFO

NOTES

1. CollegeBoard. "Average Estimated Undergraduate Budgets, 2018–19," Trends in Higher Education, 2019, https://trends.collegeboard.org/college-pricing/figures-tables/average-estimated-undergraduate-budgets-2018-19.
2. Dan Caplinger, "Rising Cost of College Creating a Financial Hole for Parents, Students: Foolish Take," USA Today, June 9, 2018, https://www.usatoday.com/story/money/personalfinance/budget-and-spending/2018/06/09/rising-cost-of-college-financial-hole/35439339.
3. Camilo Maldonado, "Price of College Increasing Almost 8 Times Faster Than Wages," *Forbes*, July 24, 2018, https://www.forbes.com/sites/camilomaldonado/2018/07/24/price-of-college-increasing-almost-8-times-faster-than-wages/#4bbdc8da66c1.
4. Tom Lindsay, "New Report: The U.S. Student-Loan Debt Crisis Is Even Worse Than We Thought," *Forbes*, May 24, 2018, https://www.forbes.com/sites/tomlindsay/2018/05/24/new-report-the-u-s-student-loan-debt-crisis-is-even-worse-than-we-thought/#69058f55e438.

5. Katie Lobosco, "Starting Salary for the Class 2018: $50,390," CNN Money, May 14, 2018, https://money.cnn.com/2018/05/14/pf/college/class-of-2018-starting-salary/index.html.

6. Delece Smith-Barrow and Josh Moody, "10 College Majors with the Lowest Starting Salaries," *U.S. News & World Report*, February 17, 2019, https://www.usnews.com/education/best-colleges/slideshows/10-college-majors-with-the-lowest-starting-salaries?onepage.

7. Susannah Snider, "Tax-Filing in 2019: What's My Tax Bracket?" *U.S. News & World Report*, January 11, 2019, https://money.usnews.com/money/personal-finance/taxes/articles/whats-my-tax-bracket.

8. "Official USDA Food Plans: Cost of Food at Home at Four Levels, U.S. Average, April 2019," United States Department of Agriculture, May 2019, https://fns-prod.azureedge.net/sites/default/files/resource-files/CostofFoodApr2019.pdf.

9. Geoff Williams, "How to Estimate Utility Costs," *U.S. News & World Report*, January 17, 2019, https://money.usnews.com/money/personal-finance/spending/articles/how-to-estimate-utility-costs.

10. "America's 2018 Rental Market in Review: Renters Finally Get Relief: Annual Rent Report, National Rent Trends 2018–2019," Abodo, January 1, 2019, https://www.abodo.com/blog/2018-annual-rent-report/.

11. Bureau of Transportation Statistics, "Average Cost of Owning and Operating an Automobile," United States Department of Transportation, https://www.bts.gov/content/average-cost-owning-and-operating-automobile.

12. "Average Car Insurance Rates by Age," CarInsurance.com, November 27, 2018, https://www.carinsurance.com/average-rates-by-age.aspx.

13. "2017 Student Loan Debt and Housing Report: Survey Respondent Demographics," CNBC.com, http://fm .cnbc.com/applications/cnbc.com/resources/editorialfiles /2018/03/29/student-loan-page4.pdf.

14. "America's 2018 Rental Market in Review."

15. "Report on the Economic Well-Being of U.S. Households in 2016 – May 2017," Board of Governors of the Federal Reserve System, June 14, 2017. https://www.federalreserve .gov/publications/2017-economic-well-being-of-us -households-in-2016-education-debt-loans.htm.

16. "America's 2018 Rental Market in Review."

17. Bureau of Transportation Statistics, "Average Cost of Owning and Operating an Automobile."

18. "John M. Vincent and Nate Parsons, "Average Used Car Loan Interest Rates in July 2019," U.S. News & World Report, July 3, 2019, https://cars.usnews.com/cars-trucks /average-used-car-loan-interest-rates.

19. Bureau of Transportation Statistics, "Average Cost of Owning and Operating an Automobile."

20. Megan Leonhardt, "Over a Third of College Students Already Have Credit Card Debt," CNBC.com, June 2, 2019, https://www.cnbc.com/2019/05/31/over-a-third-of -college-students-have-credit-card-debt.html.

21. Brad Tuttle, "$47 a Month? Why You're Probably Paying Double the 'Average' Cell Phone Bill, *Time*, October 18, 2012, http://business.time.com/2012/10/18/47-a-month -why-youre-probably-paying-double-the-average-cell -phone-bill/.

22. Susan Tompor, "Millennials Are So Buried in Debt They Can't Buy into American Dream of Owning a Home," *USA Today*, March 14, 2019, https://www.usatoday.com /story/money/personalfinance/2019/03/14/student-loan -debt-crushes-millennials-car-home-buying-american- dream/3103065002/.

23. "Report to Congressional Requesters: Public Service Loan Forgiveness," United States Government Accountability Office, September 2018, https://www.gao.gov/assets/700 /694304.pdf.

24. Annie Nova, "Just 96 of 30,000 People Who Applied for Public Service Loan Forgiveness Actually Got It," CNBC .com, September 21, 2018, https://www.cnbc.com/2018 /09/21/the-education-department-data-shows-how-rare -loan-forgiveness-is.html.

25. Farran Powell, "What You Need to Know About College Tuition Costs," *U.S. News & World Report*, September 19, 2018, https://www.usnews.com/education/best-colleges /paying-for-college/articles/what-you-need-to-know -about-college-tuition-costs.

26. CollegeBoard. "Tuition and Fees and Room and Board over Time," Trends in Higher Education, 2019, https: //trends.collegeboard.org/college-pricing/figures-tables /tuition-fees-room-and-board-over-time.

27. "Fact Sheet: Focusing Higher Education on Student Success," U.S. Department of Education, July 27, 2015, https://www.ed.gov/news/press-releases/fact-sheet-focusing -higher-education-student-success#_ftn10.

28. Jim Clifton, "The World's Broken Workplace," Gallup, June 13, 2017, https://news.gallup.com/opinion /chairman/212045/world-broken-workplace.aspx.

29. Nicole Pelletiere, "Mile-Long Pizza Breaks Guinness World Record, Slices Help Feed Homeless," ABC News, June 22, 2017, https://abcnews.go.com/Lifestyle/mile -long-pizza-breaks-guinness-world-record-slices/ story?id=48180782.

30. Duke TIP, https://tip.duke.edu.

31. CollegeBoard. "SAT Suite of Assessments: Inside the Test," 2019, https://collegereadiness.collegeboard.org/psat-8-9 /inside-the-test?excmpid=mtg431-st-1-gd.

32. "How Peers Can Push Each Other for Improvement," Jostens Renaissance Education, February 10, 2017, https://www.jostensrenaissance.com/peermotivation.

33. Eric Hoover, "An Ultra-Selective University Just Dropped the ACT/SAT. So What?" *The Chronicle of Higher Education*, June 14, 2018, https://www.chronicle.com /article/An-Ultra-Selective-University/243678.

34. Harvard College Admissions & Financial Aid, "What We Look For," Harvard University, 2019, https://college .harvard.edu/admissions/application-process/what-we-look.

35. Lynn O'Shaughnessy, "8 Things You Should Know about Sports Scholarships," CBS News, September 20, 2012, https://www.cbsnews.com/news/8-things-you-should -know-about-sports-scholarships/.

36. "Extracurricular Participation and Student Engagement," National Center for Education Statistics, June 1195, https://nces.ed.gov/pubs95/web/95741.asp.

37. AnneMarie Mannion, "Participation in Student Activities Linked to Academic Success," *Chicago Tribune*, March 18 2016, https://www.chicagotribune.com/suburbs/la-grange /news/ct-dlg-student-activities-tl-0324-20160317-story.html.

38. CollegeBoard. "Guide to the 2018 SAT/ACT Concordance," https://collegereadiness.collegeboard.org /pdf/guide-2018-act-sat-concordance.pdf.

39. Anna Aldric, "Average ACT Score for 2018, 2017, 2016, and Earlier Years," PrepScholar.com, November 4, 2018, https://blog.prepscholar.com/average-act-score -for-2015-2014-2013-and-earlier-years.

40. "What's a Good ACT Score?" Kaplan, https://www .kaptest.com/study/act/whats-good-act-score/.

41. "Reasons to Take Your Senior Year," SparrowsPoinths .bcps.org, https://sparrowspoinths.bcps.org/UserFiles /Servers/Server_4203545/File/Counseling%20Docs /reasons%20to%20take%20math%20senior%20year.pdf.

42. BigFuture, "The Facts About Applying Early: Is It Right for You?" CollegeBoard, 2019, https://bigfuture .collegeboard.org/get-in/applying-101 /the-facts-about-applying-early-is-it-right-for-you.
43. BigFuture, "Early Decision and Early Action Calendar," CollegeBoard, 2019, https://bigfuture.collegeboard .org/get-in/applying-101/early-decision-and-early -action-calendar.
44. "Clep," CollegeBoard, 2019, https://clep.collegeboard.org /earn-college-credit/practice.
45. Counseling@NYU Staff, "Gap Year Basics: How Taking a Year Off Increases the Ceiling for Students," NYU: Steinhardt, June 23, 2017, https://counseling.steinhardt .nyu.edu/blog/gap-year-after-high-school/.
46. John Ortberg, *Soul Keeping*, (Grand Rapids, Michigan: Zonderan, 2014) 49.
47. "Colleges that Produce the Most CEOs," Kittleman Blog, October 15, 2018, https://www.kittlemansearch.com /news-blog/colleges-that-produce-the-most-ceos/.

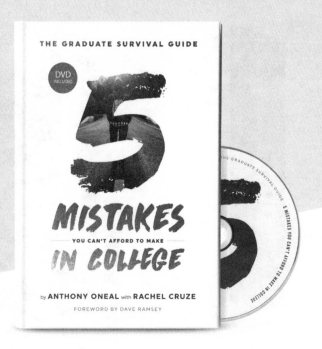

Do not go into debt! Go to a school you can afford and pick a major you will use. Robert F.

MY WIFE AND I SAVED
COLLEGE. THEY WENT TO
FOR A COUPLE YEARS AT
UNIVERSITY. THEY GRADUA

OUR TEENAGERS ARE WORKING HARD TO SAVE FOR SCHOOL AND APPLY FOR SCHOLARSHIPS. THEY WILL NOT MAKE THE SAME STUDENT LOAN MISTAKES I DID!
— MARK M.

WE STARTED
SAVINGS ACCOUN
OUR KIDS WHEN
YOUNG. BETWEEN
SCHOLARSHIPS TH
WE'LL HAVE ENO
ALL FOUR YEARS O

I WORKED MY WAY THROUGH COLLEGE AND NOW HAVE THE SAME TEACHING CERTIFICATE AS EVERYONE ELSE — BUT NO STUDENT LOANS. I DIDN'T EXPERIENCE THE COLLEGE LIFESTYLE, BUT I WOULD HAPPILY TRADE FOUR YEARS OF FUN FOR A LIFETIME WITHOUT STUDENT LOAN PAYMENTS. — CHRISTINE W.

I worked
college ar
f
debt-fre
but any
when y
and fo

I have no student loans thanks to a wonderful community college. Now I work as a NICU RN making the exact same salary as my coworkers who are still paying off thousands of dollars of debt for the very same degree.
— Jordan P.

You can totally do this without debt! Our child each received scholarsh They lived at home and part time. We paid half their tuition and books paid the other half. And walked away with a deg and zero student loans
Audrey C